PORTLAND
QUEER
TALES OF THE ROSE CITY

PORTLAND QUEER: TALES OF THE ROSE CITY

Published by LIT STAR PRESS
P.O. Box 42522
Portland, OR 97242

First edition, First printing: June, 2009
ISBN 10: 1-934620-65-3
ISBN 13: 978-1-934620-65-6

Cover and book design by Ariel Gore
Cover photo by Charles Fenno Jacobs, National Archives, 1944
Title page and back page illustrations by Annie Murphy
Section illustrations by Sarah Gottesdiener

Printed in Portland, Oregon by Eberhardt Press
Distributed by Microcosm: www.microcosmpublishing.com

PORTLAND QUEER

TALES OF THE ROSE CITY

edited by ARIEL GORE

illustrations by ANNIE MURPHY and SARAH GOTTESDIENER

LIT STAR PRESS

CONTENTS

FOR SERVICE AND DEVOTION

THEN SOMETIMES THIS FEELING OF HOME

Introduction

It's a boy," the ultrasound technician says, looking first at me, then at my teenage daughter, then at Fabulosa, sort of quizzically, like *Who are all these people?*

My straight friends call Portland the land of Lesbos, but at the clinic where I go for prenatal check-ups and at the hospital they keep asking: "Who is Fabulosa?" and "Why is she here?" and "What kind of birth control are you planning to use after the baby's born?"

None of the receptionists or practitioners seem to care when we explain that we're gay. They totally tolerate us. But I wish they'd stop asking.

"Can't you just put a pink triangle on my chart or something?" I finally suggest.

The midwife looks down at her boots. "Sorry," she says.

"Now, are we going to get you fitted for an IUD?" a nurse asks after the baby's born.

"No," I say. "I'm just planning to stay away from turkey basters for a while."

"Oh. I see." She nods down at my chart. "Oh. All right."

At the pediatrician's office a month later, the nurse wants to know if I'm the baby's grandmother. Fair enough. At thirty-seven, I'm old enough to be a grandmother. But then I realize she thinks I'm the grandmother because she thinks I'm Fabulosa's mother. And Fabulosa is thirty-five. I'm starting to get irritated. I mean, is it really *so* weird for a baby to have two moms?

Our friend Lois makes the baby a T-shirt that says, *My Other Mother is Also a Lesbian*. Perhaps this will clarify our family structure.

In the meantime, I turn my attention to more pressing matters: Raising kids and making books. I dream up *Portland Queer* late one night as I'm nursing the baby and scarfing leftover pizza from SubRosa. When the baby falls asleep, I send out a call for submissions. The guidelines are simple. I'm looking for first-person narratives by queer writers about queer characters in Portland, Oregon.

According to the Census Bureau, Portland isn't just one of the greenest city in America, it's also one of the gayest. Which is why it seems weird that we need the clarifying T-shirt. But we do.

A few days later, we get a sitter and head out to the queer dance party at Holocene.

"How long has it been since we've been out just the two of us," Fabulosa asks the road in front of us.

We're happy to be out, happy to be sipping Greyhounds, happy to see Sirius pouring them. Everyone knows that Sirius is one of the best bartenders in town, but this coke-head dyke across from me scowls when he brings us the second round. "Can't we have some *wimmin* servers around here?"

And I say "Listen, bitch, how about some goddamn solidarity? 'Cause Sirius probably isn't here serving you for his health."

And I realize that's one reason I wanted to put this book

together. *For some goddamn solidarity.* Because sometimes I think we get to feeling so privileged—like we can start turning against each other just for the hell of it. Northwest vs. Southeast vs. North vs. Southwest vs. Northeast. *You know where you belong.* And if you don't, someone will soon tell you. Gay bartender vs. lesbian coke head vs. queer mama vs. female-identified vs. "it's a boy" on the ultrasound screen.

I wanted to put this book together because the queer voices in Portland so often seem to me simultaneously intrinsic and outsider. And there's something compelling in that contradiction.

Portland is a queer magnet, a place where hometown kids come out without any old-school coming-out drama at all. And Portland is alienating and phobic, a place where the rain keeps us in our houses until we've painted the kitchen three new shades of bright and then drags us out to the bars to recover from the fumes.

Within all these contradictions, there's also common experience. In a world that tries to divide us further and further from each other, I want to see our threads woven together. In a town that's literally separated by rivers and bridges, there are rich stories and town-made legends to be known.

The true tales and likely stories that arrived in my mailbox after I sent out that call for submissions made me feel at once more at home in Portland and more like I didn't know the place at all. And maybe that's the nature of community sometimes: To feel a part of something good and bigger than ourselves and, at the same time, alone and sort of freakish.

"To queer is to destabilize the norm," my scholar friend tells me when I ask what that word means, anyway. "To queer is to make identity, gender, sexuality, family, and community moving targets."

I liked that, but I still felt overwhelmed by all the submissions. *Who was I to attempt such a huge project?* I can't represent Portland. Or queer. Or anything much beyond myself. A hundred thousand lives being lived at different intersections and in different psychic spaces. But as I read story after story, a greater story began to take shape. Not one that needed to represent all of queer Portland, but a story that wanted to be told all the same. At once a love letter to the city and a dream of escape.

queer [kweer] *adjective*, -er, -est, *verb*, *noun* **1.** strange or odd from a conventional viewpoint; unusually different; singular: a queer notion of justice. **2.** of a questionable nature or character; suspicious; shady. **3.** not feeling physically right or well; giddy, faint, or qualmish: to feel queer.

And maybe that's why I wanted to put this book together. Because I was feeling queer. And maybe that's the way we're meant to feel sometimes—giddy, faint, qualmish—like falling. Like love. Destabilizing. Moving targets. Like a part of the whole and at the same time outside of it. First person. We who are always running away and looking for home.

Ariel Gore
Portland, 2009

LOVE AND OTHER SAD, SPARKLY THINGS

PDXOX
David Ciminello

C hasing kites through Washington Park is something the cute guys do when they're bored. Sometimes the kites get snagged in the test garden of roses and become a tangle of shredded rag bits, broken balsa, crushed petals, and loose thorns.

Sometimes the kites fly high.

The beautiful ("I'm straight," he always says) waiter at Caffe Mingo, next to the restaurant where I serve, waters his guests in the outdoor café. He pours from his pitcher, weaving his way around the seven tables. A thick-veined wrist, the one with the Zappo Rip Curl Bronx watch strapped around it, flies from water glass to water glass. He's still got a bit of the boy about him, hair cropped like an early Kennedy, but the pout's all Monroe. Plump lips that dance when he smiles. *Happy Birthday, Mr. President.* We often share a cigarette around the corner in front of the dry cleaners. We blow smoke wreathes at the power lines and drop ash into the *Please Don't Lean On the Flower Boxes.* The fog from our burning tobacco does little to mask the pull of the promise he always dangles in front of me. Like a noose.

13

"If I make more than you tonight you have to suck my dick," he says.

"What if *I* make more than *you*?"

"Then you have to suck it twice."

He assumes I will, if given the opportunity. Drop to my knees and beg the way I sometimes do with strange men in the booths at Fantasy Video.

After our night of service toil and tip taking, we wander through the rain like Pepe the Ringmaster and one of his silly circus clowns. We stroll down to Voodoo Doughnut for two Dirty Snowballs, a coffee with cream, and a tall glass of cold milk.

"I'm not gonna be a waiter the rest of my life," I tell him. "It's just not gonna happen."

"OK," he says. He pushes a greasy little dough pillow topped with Cocoa Puffs into his Marilyn mouth and smiles.

"The thing about this town," I say, "is that it can swallow you whole."

His eyebrows do a dirty little Groucho dance. "I like the sound of that."

I ignore the flirt and forge ahead. "A person can get stuck here," I say. "And never find his way home."

I mean home like Dorothy's home. Like somewhere over the rainbow home. Emerald City. A date with the scarecrow that turns serious. A brain. A kiss. Then a click of my heels and a quick trip back to the farm.

Next to us the doughnut carousel spins.

"What are you gonna do if you don't wait tables?" Mingo asks.

"I got big plans," I say.

"More than a mile high," he says. "A regular flight into outer space." He waves his hands in the air and rolls his eyes.

Then his face settles into a kind of dark little puddle. "Take me with you," he says.

"Really?"

"As long as I can parachute back down."

"Always good to have an escape hatch."

Oyster-colored skies stretch over Portland, a constant reminder. *I was here before you*, the rain whispers. *I was here when the dinosaurs strolled to the ocean, I was here when the Japs were carted away, and I'll be here when you're long gone.*

I don't know why I came to this city. It's been three years and I still feel as lost as the day I arrived.

Outside, after the doughnuts, a hard rain pelts the awning over our heads. Mingo lights two Nat Shermans, sucks until both tips turn red, and hands one over. His fingers look double jointed, the nails bitten down, and I wonder why I never noticed this before. We pop lazy smoke rings into the rain and he tells me he's not gonna be a waiter forever, either. "Even if I am failing college," he says. He flicks his butt to the ground and, drunk on nicotine and fried dough, tells me he sometimes thinks about kissing a man.

"Maybe one day I'll let you kiss me," I say.

"I might do it," he says.

I can't tell if he's mocking me. And I don't want to ask.

He smiles his Mingo smile. "I gotta go," he says, and disappears into the wet.

Sipping coffee at the Starbucks on 23rd Avenue, where every color in the rainbow flag hangs out (twinks, bears, silver daddies), I think about New York—where I came from—and a cartoon bubble above my head fills with broken pavement, Circle Line boats, and roach coach falafels. I see Billy from the Empire Diner laugh. I hear Tim tell me it's over. Then the trees outside the gaybuck windows flutter and, before they completely call me back, I wonder what it might be like to leave this green PDX filled with earth-conscious growers.

"My girlfriend doesn't like to fuck," Mingo says the next night.

We are downing grapefruit margaritas at M Bar. "And when she does," he says, "she only tolerates me." He slides his tongue along the salted rim of his glass. "I'm not getting enough," he says. "And I'm bored."

It's always through the fumes of alcohol that these little revelations arrive. Like store display Christmas packages—all sugar shiny on the outside, but hollow and empty when ripped open.

"Don't you ever want to fall in love?" the silly server who works with me on Friday nights asks.

"I am in love," I say to the crude tattoo on her left shoulder—*Angelo* in inky green grammar school graffiti.

"That waiter next door is never gonna love you back," she says.

The first sunny day of spring, Mingo and I claim the bocce box from Park Kitchen. We wander over to the grassy knolls across the street where dirt courts interrupt the green like mini landing strips. In daylight, away from work, Mingo looks tired. "I'm not used to being up this early," he says.

"It's noon," I say.

"Fuck you," he says.

"Only if I win."

"And if I win?"

"I get to fuck you twice."

We whistle when we score and yell when we waste a shot.

The sun makes the sand on the court look white. Bits of stone glint in the bright. The bocce balls clank.

"Come on, old man," Mingo says and cracks my ball away to kiss the pallino. "Let's see if you can beat that."

I knock his kiss to the left and he calls a quick time out. He kicks his shoes to the ground, yanks his socks off, and rolls up his pants. "I'll do better this way," he says. The calves of his legs are dusted with a dark down, a sharp contrast to his bare forearms. The fur on his legs, the mole next to his left ankle, and the blush of his feet in the dirt all work to distract me. I lose.

"You ever do it with a girl?" he asks over chicken tacos at ¿Por Qué No?

I tell him about the time I tried to screw my high school girlfriend.

"What do you mean you *tried*?" he asks.

"We were interrupted by my grandmother," I lie.

"Too bad," he says.

"Too bad for who?"

I'm tired of Portland pastas tossed with toadstool mushrooms and fiddlehead ferns. It's awful, fussy stuff. Guppy-sized portions lost on big ceramic plates. I pine for pizza at Totonno Napolitano—a Coney Island pie with the works. Hot slices chased by a cold Coke.

My phone rings. "I broke up with my girlfriend," Mingo says. "Wanna hang out tonight?"

"Sure," I say.

That afternoon, I let the sun take me all the way to Rooster Rock. Cock Rock where the men get naked in the open air and sometimes fool around. I spread my towel on the dirt like E. M. Forster's Charlotte Bartlett pressing her mackintosh square into Italian grass and shuck my clothes. I lie back and salute the sun. In the air above me the face of Mingo appears and hovers. He fills the blue and white with a wink and smile. "My girlfriend only tolerates me. I'm so bored. Wanna hang out?"

Riding my bike over the Burnside Bridge in a cool drizzle, I skid under the white neon stag with the happy tail (Made in Portland). The Willamette rides high. It's a steady push of silt and debris. The current makes me feel like I want to box instead of beg for a kiss. But there are no Fight Clubs in Portland.

That's a dirty little lie. A dangerous literary pose.

At the corner of SE 29th and Salmon I wrap my bike lock around a mangled tree. Mingo's house is a sad two-story Greek revival with wilted rain gutters and a haunted-looking garden. I expect Edie Beale in one of her revolutionary costumes to appear as I pick my way to the front porch and press the dented buzzer. Inside, I hear an apartment door swing open. "Up here," Mingo calls.

I follow the scent of cheap cologne and stale Chinese take out up to the first landing. "Tell me that's not your perfume," I say.

"Fuck you," he says.

The main room of his place is huge. A honey-colored hardwood floor holds a double mattress, two frayed armchairs, a guitar, and an old flip-top Victrola. At the base of a fake fireplace sits a tall stack of cardboard covered twelve-inch vinyl. The Three Dog Night. Some Dylan. The Beatles. Lesley Gore. On top of the stack sits a single wrapped condom. And a bottle of lube.

"Quite a collection," I say.

"I'm a freak for this kind of stuff," he says.

I'm not sure where to sit.

"Can we get naked?" he says.

"OK," I say.

He unwraps himself a lot quicker than he did at the bocce court, not stopping at the shoes and socks. He rips off his pants. Then the underwear. The shirt flies over his head.

No disappointing Christmas package here. A grand prize stands at the bottom of his Cracker Jack box. There's a curve to the shaft of his dick and a mushroom shaped head any forest fairy would be proud to pluck. A thick treasure trail climbs up his stomach. It forks at his sternum and encircles his nipples—dark ovals, like pennies flattened on a MAX track. The rest of him is not what I imagined at all. A wounded-looking mollusk-shaped scar rests under his left collarbone. His ribcage expands and contracts in a crooked way. He helps me get out of my clothes and I want to give him a hug. Pull him into my arms and tell him it's all gonna be OK. But like Funny Girl, I hold my roses high and chug past my Statue of Liberty. I take all I can get. And he gives it to me. He even kisses back. "Let me do it," he says when I begin to take care of myself. There's no racing around the bends here. It's a long, slow ride along the river. He takes his time before he rips the condom open with his teeth. The Kennedy dimples wink when he spits away the foil. "Come here," he says. He touches me like I imagine a girl might as he rolls the condom down my stiff dick.

"Are you sure you want to do this?" I ask.

"Yes," he says. I try not to push too hard, but he pushes back and says, "please."

When we're done, he gives me a pinch on the hip, hops out of bed and strolls over to the fireplace where, more like the Marble Faun than an injured-looking young soldier, he leans on one leg to light a cigarette.

"My girlfriend called this morning," he says.

"Oh, yeah?" I say.

"She wants to get back together."

"What are you gonna do?" I ask.

"Make her suffer," he says. "Then take her back."

I Wear the Pants
Dexter Flowers

O
K, I'm really nervous to tell you this, but I used the word *whore* in a new song and I wanna know if you think it's offensive." I lowered my head, waiting for my roommate's response.

Joey paused.

I took his silence as a cue to recite my controversial lyrics. "It goes: *You like my bleach-stained towels, and I like that you dress like a whore!*"

Joey looked at me with calm brown eyes. "That could offend people in the sex work industry, why not use a different word?"

I was disappointed. My feelings are always obvious on me—like ladies' perfume. My emotions seep out my pores, making my secrets public. "I don't want to offend whores, but it's positive toward the whores, see, it says that I *like* that you dress like a whore."

"Sex worker!" Joey corrected me. "And what does a whore dress like? You're stereotyping."

I looked at Joey's attractive little Mohawk, the dark beard that framed his light brown face. I strategized about how I might win his approval. His tattooed arms were crossed firmly over his chest. I stared at the tattoo of an anchor with his cat's name on it. If I could get those arms to uncross, I might have a chance.

I thought of Joey as my authority when it came to PC behavior. Since moving to Portland, I'd made it my mission not to be ignorant. I'd already given up the words *lame, retard* and *gypped* (who knew it referred to the idea that Gypsies rip people off?) "But I thought Gypsies *did* steal," I said to Joey when he told me to avoid using the word.

"Yes, for survival, but it's still a generalization. Do you think *all* Gypsies are thieves?" Joey eyed me suspiciously, challenging my mind to new frontiers—like I was a college student on my first hit of acid with some hippie professor in the 1960s.

"No, I don't think *all* Gypsies are thieves." I said it proudly, like I'd taken a political stand.

Joey was satisfied—I could tell by the glint in his eyes. I desperately wanted to see that glint again, so I searched my mind for a word that rhymed with *whore* because the next line ended with the word *store*. "Well, I guess I could say, *I like that you dress like an encore?* Or *a roar?*" I hated it. I wanted the "whore" back so bad.

I was still thinking about my lyrics a few days later when Joey and the rest of our friends planned their weekly trip to sing karaoke at the Silverado.

"Can I come?" I piped up.

"Oh there's no way they'll let you in, Dexter, You don't even have a fake ID," my friend Gertrude said. "They're tough at the door there." She had a mother hen look on her face as she tried to convince me not to leave the house.

"But I look older than my age," I squeaked. I wanted her to look at me, at my obvious *maturity*. My older friends did look, getting a spectacular image of me in my pleather pants, tri-stud belt, white T-shirt that said, "sounds like a personal problem to me" across one breast, poorly-decided-upon spiky black hair, and huge Buddy Holly glasses that ate my face.

"OK, Big D., it's up to you," Caroline said. "But it's gonna suck if they turn you away." She smoothed her bleached hair in a suave and boyish way I was incapable of.

My hair wasn't meant for touching. I'd perfectly sculpted it with layers upon layers of Murray's Pomade. Anyone who dared to muss up my sticky hair sculpture would have to deal with my wrath.

One time an adorable friend of mine named Elle had given me a hug outside an old theater space on Mississippi and one of my then-pink hair spikes stabbed her in the eye. Her eye went red with tears. I walked her to the bathroom and held her soft curls away from her face as she flushed out her poor eye. Years later, I discovered there was a rumor that I'd broken Elle's heart. This explained why she'd burst into tears so abruptly.

"I'm coming with you guys," I insisted. I would not be deprived of gay karaoke. It encompassed too many fabulous things. And I'd worn my pleather pants. *What a waste if I had to stay home in them.* I imagined how cool I looked—just like the girls in Tribe 8 in their genuine leather. The pants had been too big on me, so I'd hand sewn the flimsy fabric tighter with dental floss. I wanted them that badly.

I jumped into Joey's car. We were off to meet the crew at the Silverado. But first we'd pick up his friend Lorraine. We honked outside her big haunted house on Moore Street, just off the sketchy part of Killingsworth. Next door there was this party store/suspicious looking hot dog shop with a little neon heart in the window.

Lorraine burst out the front door and down the stairs. She was all sequins and crinoline poofing out from under her fancy black dress. Her hair was long, with Bettie Page bangs and wild magenta streaks. She reminded me of things I loved: Cyndi Lauper and sparkly vaudeville costume closets. My eyes caught on her false eyelashes as she threw her lady skirt into the backseat. She smelled like vanilla candles.

"I'm Dexter, Joey's new roommate," I breathed out.

Lorraine offered me her hand and smiled.

We met Caroline and Gertrude at the door of the Silverado and our group was greeted like royalty. The door guy knew them all, and I was lumped into the bouquet of the known. He didn't ask for IDs.

"What were you guys saying about how hard it is to get in? How I'll never get past the door?" I said it all bratty, a hand on my hip, looking at Gertrude and Caroline.

"I guess we were wrong." Caroline adjusted her cowboy hat and walked ahead of me to find a table.

I sat down next to Lorraine, watched her stir her straw in her whiskey Coke and bat those huge eyelashes like she was Doris Day.

I would spend my meager earnings from the after-school art program where I worked to get sloshed at the Silverado. I wanted my initiation into the adult world of gay karaoke to be memorable and whiskey-soaked. My job only paid me $7.10 an hour, and I only worked twenty hours a week, but I survived. My diet consisted primarily of bread from the free bin outside the post office on Killingsworth, rice, and the vegan comfort food Joey graciously fed me. Ours was a mutually-desired relationship with codependent perks we both enjoyed. I got royally fed and Joey got to feel the pride of being an amazing cook. I loved his lentil loaf so much I'd talk about it for days—like it was a sexual experience. "Mmm, remember the lentil loaf? I can't get over it, I think about that lentil loaf all the time."

I even called in sick every few months. I'd moan to my boss: "I have explosive diarrhea." I gloated to my friends that this was the perfect excuse because no one wants to continue a conversation that begins with explosive diarrhea. And now here I was, sitting next to Lorraine at the Silverado, buying myself alcohol like I worked on Wall Street.

The bartender, who looked like a real male model, shouted "A round for my favorite people!" as he brought shots of Cuervo to our table.

"Wow!" I mouthed to Lorraine, feeling blanketed under my new elite status.

"Yeah, they LOVE us here. He always gives us free drinks. I'm not sure if he's gay or not. He definitely flirts with me at the bar." Lorraine smiled mischievously and scrunched her lips like a little kid who knows some secret information.

The KJ took his job seriously. A man in his mid-fifties, he had these fantastic business cards emblazoned with a picture of himself—with his cheesy smile and a mic in one hand. He, too, treated our clique like stars, expediting songs and showering us with compliments when he announced us to the floor. I was entranced by the drag queens—so glittery and boldly dressed like Lorraine. They sang torch songs. Older gentlemen gave me goose bumps with their heartfelt Sinatra ballads. When my song came up, I would give it my all. I studied myself in the wall of tall mirrors: There I was under the blue lights with my flashy pants, my dyed black bangs in my eyes. I wondered if I matched this place of my dreams.

"Next, we have a very special lady. Lorraine, come up here, toots! Isn't she a looker? OK, give her your attention!" The KJ loved Lorraine in a way that made her blush sweetly and look uncomfortable at the same time, like she was a cat dressed in doll clothes. My heart swelled as Lorraine started singing "Sister Christian."

I turned to Joey. "Oh, I like her!"

Joey smiled his little teeth at me. "She's really great."

By the time my song was called, I was sloshing my straw into a drink, explaining to someone I didn't know that "I moved to Portland for the *communi-tyyy*." I did feel a sense of possible grand purpose waiting for me as I waltzed up to the microphone. I had picked the Monkees song "I'm a Believer."

"I thought love was only true in fairy tales," I sang, shaking my pleather pants toward Lorraine like I was Jerry Lee Lewis. I looked at the KJ, and his face crinkled into a smile. This was encouraging. I soaked up all that external happiness and pushed it into my anxiety-ridden guts. I fell to my knees as I sang, "Ahhh, I'm in love, I'm a believer, I couldn't leave her if I tried." Still on my knees, disco ball light all over me, the applause burst forth. My knees hurt from the abrupt thump, but I stood up, brought the song home. Nipples hard with whiskey, I headed back to my friends.

"*Alriiight*, Dexter Casanova!" The KJ said.

My confidence soared. The karaoke approval, Lorraine's amused smile, the Coke and whiskey, did it really matter where my confidence was coming from? Couldn't it just matter that it was there? I had lost my seat to someone else, so I leaned forward on a chair, my ass pooched out into the Silverado air.

"Hot, hot, hot!" a man's voice came from behind. I felt full-on hands stroking the plasticky behind of my pants. I turned around to see this petite, dark-haired man dressed in beige and drinking a bottle of beer.

"Don't do that!" I commanded him, setting a great boundary. It felt good. Since moving to Portland, I'd worked hard on establishing boundaries, on speaking up for myself. I didn't wait for his response. I resumed my ass-in-the-air position. I rolled my eyes at pretty Lorraine who smiled up at me like she was also familiar with strange men trying to pet her butt. And then, to my shock and displeasure, I felt the hand again. "I SAID, don't touch me!"

"Take it easy, sweetheart. I'M GAY!" the little man shot back. He glared at me as if to say I was an *overreactor* and unjustly flattering myself.

"Just because you're gay does not give you the right to touch my butt," I insisted, sounding like a proper woman at teatime.

"Whatever! I'm GAY! GAY! GAY!" the man yelled, walking away.

With all the politically correct activism and firm stances people took in Portland, why couldn't this, too, be important? Maybe this could be *my* political and societal issue: Gay men at the Silverado thinking they have the right to make dykes into a petting zoo. I did have a tendency to overreact, but why not overreact about something I could pin to a cause? Riot girl, protector, feminist, radical no shit taker—this could be me. "I can't believe men think they have the right to touch women in public! It's just like the time I was at Sally's Beauty Supply with Violet and the guy working there touched her hair. When she moved away, he said, 'Please hon, I'm gay.'" I was on a roll. My whiskey buzz and my karaoke starlit moment were gone. My happiness had melted like candle wax, now solidifying into a real drag.

"It's uncool," Joey agreed.

Luckily, everyone was ready to go home. This time I sat in the backseat with Lorraine, who still smelled like vanilla. We'd picked up a few extra friends who needed rides home. "I feel so violated." I continued my drama. I was the innocent victim of an ass-snatching gay man with bad boundaries.

Lorraine's eyes sparkled pale blue in the red traffic light. She rested her head on my shoulder. I gulped in air as her hair trailed across my chest. "I hope *this* doesn't make you feel violated," she said softly, leaning in close and challenging me as she put her arm on my thigh.

"No, this is different," I squeaked. "This is consensual." I curled my arm around her.

"Good, I'm glad," Lorraine said, making herself more comfortable.

I tried to hang on to this shining moment. My insides were squishy and pleasant things. My arms were sturdy bike handlebars, holding someone precious.

Back home, I went into the bathroom. There were layers of punk rock history in there: A Debbie Harry poster—"Andy Warhol is Bad," dust and grime, peeling paint. I looked in the mirror and was startled. Half my face was smudged magenta from Lorraine's fresh streaks. I smiled. I liked Lorraine. I was learning things in Portland. I knew that certain words were off limits. I knew how to stand up for something I believed in. I knew how to have moments of happiness. I stared at all the hair dye on my baby face, pushed my heavy glasses up on my nose, looked and looked at my mirror reflection. I still had so much to learn.

The Strange and Highly Selective Mating Patterns of the Human Male Animal

Michael Sage Ricci

I have a confession to make. My name is Glutter and I'm a 33rd level Paladin. Seriously. I'm a videogame addict, part of a massive multiplayer online role-playing community. Go ahead and laugh now. My feelings won't get hurt.

Andy says video games are only for the truly demented, and are especially pathetic once you're past age thirty. Andy's my best friend. We get cocktails at Starky's every Monday night. Cheap cheeseburgers, too—five bucks but the bacon's extra. Andy calls my flesh and blood ordinary mundane reality The Meat World. Andy calls my videogame world my Wet Dream.

In the Wet Dream, I'm a mighty Elfin holy warrior dealing retribution for an angry god. In the Wet Dream, I am strong and silent, certain of my faith in the world and my role in the cosmos.

In the Dream, I am a woman.

I am Glutter. Hear me roar.

Where I am weak, Glutter is filled with spirit. Where I am uncertain, she is fierce. What can I say? Andy was right.

Demented and pathetic. For some it's cigarettes or booze or sex. For me, it's Glutter. Well, sex too, but mostly Glutter. She's safer.

Or so I thought.

At first my online life didn't interfere at all with the Meat World. Just a way to relax after a hard day's work. Solve puzzles, kill monsters, find treasure. Simple and direct. Life was groovy.

Until, that is, Glutter met her secret online lover.

Over two margaritas and the Bette Midler DVD playing on Starky's widescreen, I told the whole tragic story to Andy.

That night was business as usual for Glutter. Running around the Wet Dream world decked out in new pink armor, a purple glowy helmet, black thigh-high boots, and a sword that looked like a giant flaming cleaver. Sooooo gay.

Like I told Andy, there I was, raiding the Fire Ogres that had settled an abandoned coal mine in the high desolate mountain wastes of the Aragon Highlands.

Glutter ripped through the mine with simple cartoon violence, swinging her flaming cleaver. Kicking ass and taking names. The Monster's name said it all. Howlbelly. Leader of the Fire Ogres.

That's where Andy draws the line. He says I'm not allowed to use names of any videogame characters in our conversations. Only real people. Life is confusing enough.

But anyway, forget Andy, he's bitter. There I was attacking Howlbelly, I mean, the Ogre. I'm using my Holy Shield. I'm hacking away with my flaming cleaver. My Blessing of Retribution.

But the Ogre is too strong. He's too high a level. My health points are almost at zero. Just as Glutter is going to bite it, though, this long green arrow shoots into the Ogre from off to the side. Then another. And another. The Ogre falls to the stony ground, dead.

I can't believe it. I turn Glutter around to see who saved her, I mean me, saved me. No, I mean I turn Glutter around to see who saved *us*.

The dim sun of Aragon sparkled in our high red hair, glinted off the purple glowy helmet. So fierce. That's when I met him.

HearthBubble the Hunter.

Another player, another real live person sitting in a room somewhere at his computer.

Hearthbubble was Elf like me, but with fancier gear. He had to be at least level 60. Green leather jerkin with a hood and a long curved bow strapped back across his shoulders. Everything he wore had special effects, like glowing runes on the bow, and silver spellthread sewn into his collar to give bonus armor enchantments.

Hearthbubble waved. And a little word balloon appeared over his head. "Lookd like u were in trubl."

In the Wet Dream, everyone types to be as brief as possible. It's amazing how little can be said to get your point across. LOL means laugh out loud. OMG means Oh My God. WTF means What The Fuck.

"OMG" I typed "Thx for the save."

Then I typed /Shy. That's called an Emote. Anything after the slash tells your character to respond a certain way. Glutter crossed her arms and twirled her toe in the dirt, purple glowy helmet almost sheepish and looking away from HearthBubble.

"LOL" said HearthBubble. "NP." No Problem.

"Hey," he said. "MayB I can help you level fster."

That's how it started between us. It was so innocent. HearthBubble helped me finish looting the Ogre mine, and gave me all the treasure. Then he helped me track down a Giant five levels higher than me, one I never could have killed on my own. Hearthbubble was respectful, too, acting like a perfect gentleman. If my power levels were low, he gave me potions and food.

Andy said I should have just ended it there, tell HearthBubble I was a guy.

"It's not like that," I said. "It's actually sweet."

Andy just gave me that look of his, one eyebrow over his glasses.

Things with HB changed pretty quick. HB was how I started abbreviating HearthBubble's name in our chats. About two days after we met, I logged into the game and immediately got a message. "Hey Glut. What u doin? Nd help?"

HB must have added me to his friends list. Now he knew every time I logged on.

After that we met up every day. We caught the boat to TangleVine Vale together. He helped me fight the pirates of Booty Bayou. It's hard to play and type a lot at the same time, so most of the time we were silent, just running alongside each other as we fought monsters and pirates, demons and ghosts. He'd let me take the first shot then he'd attack, ending the fight in moments. We never traded our real names. When we did talk, it was mostly business.

"Watch out 4 trolls."

"Don't aggro the shaman."

"Sell that for gold at AH."

AH means AuctionHouse. HB always let me keep the treasure.

I like playing a girl. If you bat your eyelashes just right, guys will give you stuff. HB gave me a baby dragon as a pet. And a new sword, one that gave me a strength bonus and a chance to deal extra damage each time I hit. He gave me gold.

Now we're talking. Glutter got bling.

It was our third week of playing together. We were planning times to meet nightly. That's how I knew we lived in the same time zone. But I didn't have the balls to ask him where he lived. I played it cool, let him lead, call all the shots. I was careful to sound like I thought HB would expect a girl to sound. I never *said* I was a girl. But I never said I wasn't.

And the Emotes kept coming. /Shy was just the beginning. /Dance made Glutter dance around the Wet Dream world like a stripper doing a pole dance. Hands to the hip, shoulder shoulder, kick kick kick. Time it just right, so that when Glutter begins a twirl, I remove her helmet then her boots from my inventory list so onscreen it looked a little like a striptease. HB /Danced too, moving close to Glutter so everyone knew in the SilverGrove town square that we were together.

Next came /Flirt. If you type /Flirt, your on-screen character will say something funny, sometimes cruel, and always *very* gay. I mean, seriously. Someone wearing pink underpants was obviously working in the Elf development department at this game company. *Someone* had to write this shit.

HB /Flirted. His voice was high and musical and his hands waved in big arcs as he talked, spots of light glowing from his spellthread. "You know what I love about your eyes? When I look in them just right, I can see my own reflection." And, "You can stand close, just don't mess the hair." And my favorite, "Pour some sugar on me, honey-pie, and serve me for dessert!"

OK. Reality check.

I'm well aware that most online video game players are adolescent boys. Forget about the constant posturing about who's tougher and who could kick whose ass. Five minutes on the game chat and you hear "faggot" enough times to lose count. It's why Glutter sticks to herself.

But HB was no teen. In the course of two weeks I got some of his story. Marine. Late twenties. Likes videogames and Monster Trucks. It's amazing how little I had to say. He didn't seem interested in my story if I kept asking him about himself.

When I told Andy that part, he tilted back his margarita and swallowed a big gulp. He wiped his mouth with the back of his hand. "Just like a man," he said.

So, one night I was online checking my auctions at the AH to see if I made any more bling. In the chatbox: HEARTHBUBBLE HAS LOGGED ON.

"Heya," I typed. "Can u cm to the UnderTemple and help me kill the undead Dragon King?"

"Srry no time." HB typed. "Just checkin my auctions. Goin 2 a ball game 2nite."

"Is ok. NP. Who's playin?" Not that I cared. Sports were more up Andy's alley. I just wanted HearthBubble to keep chatting.

"Portland Trailblazers."

OMG. The Blazers were playing in town. Andy was going to the game.

"I live in Portland 2." I typed.

Silence in the chatbox. My mailbox button lit up and the AH bell chimed. Someone had purchased my auction of invisibility potions.

After a full minute, HB typed back.

"C ya latr."

Then: HEARTHBUBBLE HAS LOGGED OFF.

Next day came the shocker.

HB met up with me at the UnderTemple. It was business as usual, deep in the dungeon, running down a dark hall. We hadn't said anything to each other yet. We let our characters make the motions we needed to understand one another. It was all Emotes. /Wave, and /Point. We had made it through the whole temple that way, almost to the end. The only thing left to do was slay the Undead Dragon King.

Like I said, business as usual. We squared off against the King, huge dragon skull smiling pointy dragon teeth. I cast Stun Spell. My Flaming cleaver. Blessing of Retribution. But no bow and arrow, where's the godamn bow and arrow?

Onscreen, HB just stood there next to Glutter, unmoving. I was about to get creamed.

"WTF?!?!?" I typed.

"Oops." HB typed. "Got2 go. My girlfrnd jst got home!"

Girlfriend.

I stopped fighting. My fingers actually stopped moving on the keyboard. The dragon's head pulled back and opened its mouth of teeth. A blast of flame just as HB waved to me. The green hood. The leather jerkin. Longbow. Before his waving body disappeared from my screen, he Emoted one more thing.

/Kiss.

HB put his hand to his mouth and from the screen a long wet smooching kiss sound kissed out at me and he disappeared leaving me in dragon flame.

HEARTHBUBBLE HAS LOGGED OFF.

The dragon chomped into me. The damage was insane. I couldn't lift my sword. Couldn't cast a spell. I died and had to start over from the Graveyard.

OMG WTF. Only a few weeks playing as a girl and already I'm the other woman.

I wish it ended there. I didn't know what to do. I should have taken Andy's advice to drop the whole bizarre thing freako you know you're really worrying me here.

I tried to restrain myself, give it a few days before logging back in. Let things cool off. But as soon as I logged in, right away there he was in my chatbox.

"QQ," HB typed.

QQ means 2 sad eyes looking down.

"Y R U sad?" I typed.

"Mssd U."

"O rly?"

"No srsly, I did."

This was becoming kind of bizarre, even by my standards. Yes, I was pretending to be something I wasn't. But my feelings were real. I was loosening up with him, joking around. And the way I felt whenever I saw HB's name in my chatbox. I hadn't felt like this in the Meat World in a long time.

"Srry I abandnd u." HB typed.

Dangerous territory. It was actually appealing at first, the ambiguity of what we were doing together. Were we flirting? Was this online dating? It was some strange gift the universe dropped in my lap. Some glimpse into a heterosexual world I had never been a part of. The way HB was with me, it felt old-fashioned in some silly and sweet kind of way.

Andy was right. Pathetic.

Best to end it quick. Up the ante and scare him off.

"What about ur girlfriend?" I typed.

HB was ready for me though. There was no hesitation.

"What she don't know won't hurt her."

And there on the screen, right there in the SilverGrove Town Square, HB appeared in front of Glutter. He must have tracked me through the friends list. He /Smiled. He /Waved. He /Danced. Emote. Emote. Emote. HB started a Disco move, hands up and pointing, hips thrusting towards me.

All right. All or nothing. Here goes.

/Dance, I Emoted. Glutter started her strip pole tease in

time with HB's Disco hip thrust. Hands to the hip, shoulder shoulder, kick kick kick.

"Let's meet then," I typed. "For real. In the Meat World."

HB kept dancing. Glutter kept dancing. Please say no. Please just log off and never talk with me again.

The chatbox lit up.

"Where should we meet?"

OMFG. What was I thinking? I had no idea what he was really like. For God's sake, he was a Marine, he could kill me. I should have just moved my mouse cursor over to the logout button. The whole Wet Dream would have faded to the login screen.

But no. It was too far gone for that.

I typed it quick. No remorse. Keep upping the ante. Playing chicken with an oncoming train. The headlights were close, but I wasn't going to bail first. If I stopped to think about it, the fear would never have let the notion past my fingertips.

Seize the day and to hell with consequences.

"Ever heard of Starky's?" I typed.

I hoped he had, hoped he knew it was a Gay bar.

"No, give me the address. Can we meet 2nite? My girlfriend will be at school until 11."

There was no way I could imagine myself meeting HB. No ending I could foresee that didn't end in something terribly strange or even painful.

"Sure." I typed. "7 PM." I gave him the address on Stark Street. Then I hit the logoff button without waiting for a response.

Now let me tell you something. In my heart of hearts, I am a stinking no good coward. Sad to say, I didn't care that HB had a girlfriend. I just didn't want to get beat up. All afternoon, all I could think about was not going.

I would have chickened out for sure if Andy hadn't called.

"It's Monday, remember? I'll be there with you. We'll sit in the corner of the bar and just wait for the first horny camouflaged completely unironic straight guy to walk in the door. View it as a social experiment, or one of those nature documentaries you love. *The strange and highly selective mating patterns of the human male animal.*"

Then, after a pause, Andy added, "Is unironic a word?"

6:45 p.m. Monday night. Me and Andy walked through the blue swinging door into Starky's. No one sat at the bar, we got our regular seats in the corner. We could see the whole bar and most of the front room. The lottery machines. The Keno digital readout. The wall mounted widescreen TV showing Bette Midler singing her tits off.

Two Margaritas and an extra smile from Pat the bartender when he handed Andy his drink. "Pretty dead tonight."

Andy lowered his eyes, suddenly shy.

Across from where we sat, just sitting there on the other side of the bar, was a drink. Looked like Scotch in the glass. Looked lonely, half drunk, waiting for someone to come back and pick it up.

6:52 p.m. Someone opened the blue swinging door and stepped past the entryway into the bar. I've met him before, Craig or Chris something. Blue jeans. Button down white shirt. He sat exactly halfway between me and the half drunk glass of Scotch. Craig or Chris nodded at Pat and ordered a micro-brew, something local.

It's not that Craig/Chris is bad looking or anti-social or seriously deformed. There's just something strange about him. He's definitely jumpy, a little too nervous, like he's desperate all the time. People sense it too, tend to steer clear of him.

Believe me, nothing kills a hard-on like desperation.

6:57. Mike the Dyke came in. Born and raised and lived

her whole life in Southeast Portland, older than dirt, and still kicking. She probably wasn't as old as she looked, but nicotine had turned her hair and skin yellow-white. Mike used to like to come to Starky's and smoke cigarillos and drink Pabst and play Keno, but now she comes to drink Pabst and play Keno and bitch about how she can't smoke cigarillos in the bar anymore. Mike sat down in the seat next to the empty glass of Scotch. Pat the bartender didn't say a word, popped open a can of Pabst and put it down in front of her.

7:04. Andy got a call on his cell phone. Some hot date had come through. Pat the Bartender was wiping glasses near us and looked over at Andy who got that shy look again and lowered his voice. Pat the Bartender just smiled.

Andy clicked his cell phone shut and gave me that look, the eyebrow raised over his glasses. "Don't hate me 'cause I'm beautiful," he said, and stood up pushing the barstool back with his knees. He slammed the rest of his margarita into his mouth, not spilling a drop. "Hate me 'cause I'm getting laid and you aren't. Sorry, gotta go."

Andy slapped a ten onto the counter. "Keep the change," he said, and Pat the Bartender still had that smile.

"I work until midnight," Pat said.

"Andy, you can't—" I tried to grab for his coat, his sleeve, anything. "Don't abandon me."

Andy leaned close and kissed my forehead. I could smell margarita, cigarette smoke. His lips were wet and warm. "You can't abandon what you never had. You got yourself into this, you'll be fine. Just be careful. Remember, this is Meat World. If he kills you, you don't get to start over at the Graveyard."

"Funny Andy, really funny, come *on* don't leave."

But it was no use. Andy winked at me, looked up at Pat and smiled his shy little smile. Then he was through the swinging blue door and gone.

The strange and highly selective mating patterns of the human male animal.

Shit.

Pat the bartender mixed another margarita without looking at me or asking me if I wanted one. He set it down in front of me, picked up the money Andy left for him.

7:12. The men's room door opened and the owner of the half drunk Scotch made his way back to his seat at the bar next to Mike the Dyke.

Mike the Dyke was oblivious, reading the Keno display and checking off numbers on her ticket.

The Scotch guy was a big guy, I mean really big, at least 250, easy. His muscles had muscles. Beefy, and a huge belly, veins sticking up from his arms. Shaved head and three-day white scruff.

"Thought we lost you," Pat the Bartender said to Muscles. "Was about to send a search party in after you."

"It's the new meds," Muscles said. He sipped his Scotch slow.

7:17 The blue swinging door swung open. HearthBubble the Hunter stepped through the entryway into the bar.

I'd know him anywhere. He was Emoting all over the place.

/Horny. /Macho. Sunglasses. A black and red ball cap backwards on his buzzcut head. Fresh shaved squared jaw. Washboard stomach under his tight black T-shirt. NO FEAR in white letters.

Andy had him pegged. HB was wearing camouflage pants. It was the new camouflage, not the old green and olive and brown army kind, but the Iraq kind, khaki and sand. Completely neutral. I guess unironic really is a word.

HB stood in the doorway taking it all in: Craig/Chris and Mike the Dyke and Pat the Bartender and Muscles. When HB looked my way, I took a big gulp on the margarita like Andy would. I didn't spill a drop.

HB checked his watch, looked over at Craig/Chris again, looked at Pat the Bartender. /Nervous.

Pat was all smiles, his salt and pepper goatee and hair combed back over his ears. Sweet and sexy in a non-threatening way like any good bartender who wants to make big tips. Pat was extra friendly towards HB. He squared his hips, leaned forward onto the bar, his blue jeans ass sticking out straight behind him. Real casual. You could practically hear the porno soundtrack going off inside his head. Thump thump thump.

"Hey buddy what can I get for you?"

HB stepped forward to the bar, took off his sunglasses. Brown eyes and thick dark eyebrows. He looked French or Italian. His voice was unexpected. Soft and deep, but not sure of itself. "Uh I want a beer, let's see," HB said.

I thought he'd order Bud. But, after all, this *is* Portland. "Um a lager, but not too light, maybe an ale, something Amber maybe, with a nice hops finish."

Pat the Bartender turned quick, grabbing a glass and reaching for the taps. "I got what you need," he said. Thump thump thump.

Craig/Chris laughed, so excited he was practically shaking. Pat the Bartender laughed. Muscles rolled his eyes up then went right back to staring at HB's ass.

Pat the Bartender finished pouring the beer and set it down on the counter. He held his hand up and shook his head when HB reached for his wallet. "It's on me."

"Thanks." HB said. /Smile.

It was that smile that got us. The full lips and the perfect white teeth.

All the men at the bar, every one of us, all we could do was just stare.

And the way he reached for the beer, glass to his lips. The moment those lips touched the rim I was gone. Lost. We all were. Me and Pat and Craig/Chris and Muscles, lost in moisture and tongue, amber beer in big sloshy gulps, shaved head leaning back, shaved chin, breathing beer in, adam's apple up and down. My God the beauty. Unironic. No metaphor could contain it. The last of the beer down his throat, one last swallow and he brought the glass down, empty.

/Awe. /Lust. /Speechless.

Emote. Emote. Emote.

Muscles sipped his Scotch and who knew what was going on behind those big eyes, his impossible tan, the veins and the muscle. Pat the Bartender leaned on the counter, thump thump thump, forgetting to look cool, the dishtowel hanging from his hand. Craig/Chris's hand on the bar couldn't keep still. Touch his beer, then his wallet, then his shirt button. Lost in the moment. All of us. Lost.

HB lowered the glass, his eyes closed for a second. His hand found the counter and set the glass down.

Muscles licked his lips. Pat the Bartender didn't stand up, stayed leaning against the counter. "Let me get you another one," he said.

HB opened his eyes. That's when he really saw us. Saw us staring at him. Saw what was on our faces.

It was like one of those nature shows. Predators and their prey. A gazelle that has stumbled across a pack of hyenas.

But HB was no gazelle. You could see him getting it. Like in a cartoon, you could almost see the light bulb come on over his head. What Starky's was. What we are. How Glutter was never going to show.

The strange and highly selective mating patterns of the human male animal.

/Shock. /Revulsion. HB's eyes moved to Muscles, then

back to Pat the Bartender. Italian or French eyes on mine for just a second.

/Betrayal. I saw him in pain and didn't speak up, didn't call out to him or buy him a beer or crack a joke. He never knew it was me. I never said a word.

/Anger. HB turned from prey to predator quicker than you can say fagbash.

His hands tightened into fists. He eyed me first, but I'm no slouch. I'm not huge like Muscles, but I'm a good five-foot-ten, got some heft to me. I mean really I'm a creampuff, but I look like I'll give you a fight.

HB probably would have gone for Craig/Chris. That's what I would have done if I wanted a pushover.

Muscles saw it too. He just cleared his throat, loud enough for everyone to hear. Kept sipping his Scotch, not saying a word. HB turned towards the sound. Saw Muscles. Saw Muscles' muscles.

Muscles said it real casual, but there was no mistaking the full on righteous queen in his voice. "Ohhh, so butch. But I think you're in the wrong bar, dear."

HB opened his mouth, like to say something, who knows what, because he never said it. Iraq not withstanding, he knew a losing battle when he saw one. Gazelle versus hyena. All he could do was get the hell out of SilverGrove.

HB pushed open the blue swinging door and left a hole in the air behind him we could only sit and stare at in wonder.

Muscles talked first. He had a little smirk again at the corner of his mouth. "Well, that was certainly *interesting*. What the hell just happened?"

I answered without thinking. "A mistake."

Muscles was on it, didn't miss a beat. "*That* sounds revealing. A mistake for who?" Muscles big eyes went wider. "Enquiring minds want to know."

But Mike the Dyke saved me from having to ignore him. "Holy Jesus!" She looked up at the Keno display and then down at her card again. "I think I won!"

Pat the Bartender was looking at the hole in the air where HB had been standing. He reached under the bar and began setting shot glasses in front of him, one at a time. Five of them. He reached behind him for a bottle. "I think we could all use a drink."

It was later that week. I finally got the balls up to log back into the Wet Dream world.

I was in SilverGrove, checking my auctions. I had just bid on a new cloak, purple to match Glutter's helmet, with silver trim and a healing enchantment.

HB was across the town square. I could barely make him out above a crowd of Elves and Orcs. He was just standing there, facing me. The green hood. The longbow. The spellthread.

We stood that way for a minute or two. Neither of us moving.

I clicked on his character and typed "QQ."

The message popped right up in the chatbox.

HEARTHBUBBLE HAS PLACED YOU ON HIS IGNORE LIST.

Once you are on someone's IGNORE list, all you can do is Emote at them.

/Wave I Emoted.

Glutter's hand raised and waved.

HB started walking, a straight line towards me through the crowd in the town square.

/Spit. He spit on the ground in disgust.

If animation could tremble, Glutter would have been shaking in her enchanted boots.

Before I could turn to run away, though, the words appeared

onscreen: HEARTHBUBBLE HAS CHALLENGED YOU TO A DUEL.

WTF?

Surprised, but I didn't hesitate, not even for a second. I clicked the *accept* button. It seemed right somehow that it came to this.

DUEL BEGINS IN 3 SECONDS.

HB backed away and readied an arrow in his bow.

I cast Holy Shield. Not a second too soon. HB's long green arrows bounced off my protective force field. I was invulnerable to him for twenty more seconds. Then he would kill me.

I could fool myself. Try to defend my demented and pathetic actions. Play the victim. Tell myself I did it because being gay meant always being tricked and never being the trickster, being the bullied and never the bully. I did it because I was fed up and wanted to dish it out for once.

But that's bullshit.

The truth is like I told you.

In my heart of hearts, I am a stinking no-good coward.

The shriveled meat center at the heart of the Wet Dream illusion.

Not man enough to finish what I started.

I didn't want to fight HB. There was only one thing I could do.

/Dance.

Glutter began her striptease pole dance. Hands to the hip, shoulder shoulder, kick kick kick.

HB stopped firing his bow, waiting for the shield to drop. A crowd of Elves and Orcs was gathering around to watch the duel. /Cheering, /Applauding. "I bet that chicks a dude," someone typed in the chatbox.

I timed it just right. Each time Glutter turned, I selected a piece of clothing from her inventory list. I removed each layer, each piece of armor, deleting the item, dropping it offscreen, forever destroying it, no way of getting it back. Item by item I stripped Glutter of everything that gave her meaning, down to her red string bikini, the closest you could get to nudity in the Wet Dream world.

/Dance.
/Cry.
/Die.
Emote.
Emote.
Emote.

Ave Maria
Colleen Siviter

To this day I don't know why the nuns accepted me into the academy. My grades were poor, my entrance essay mediocre, and the interview a nightmare. My mom, using her usual questionable judgment, had brought along my one-year-old sister, who crawled around the floor and under the table until I picked her up and conducted most of the interview alternating between rocking her and bouncing her on my knee. I'd done my best to look presentable. I'd left my black flight jacket covered with band pins and patches at home, donned men's vintage polyester pants instead of my uniform ripped tights, and even combed my black bangs to the side and secured them with a bobby pin. There was nothing I could do about the combat boots. They were the only shoes I owned.

St. Mary's was the only all-girls school in Portland. I'd seen the brick building downtown, but I didn't know anyone who went there. I didn't know anything about it. All girls was all that mattered. I was sick of wasting my time at a suburban public school doing drugs, fighting with jocks, and skipping class. How could I focus on schoolwork when I was surrounded by dudes who publicly degraded women's bodies and then jacked each other off on the weekends—just to turn around and hate on fags? The hypocrisy was just too much. I was disgusted and exhausted and it was only the beginning of sophomore year.

St. Mary's was my way out. I would be leaving behind the only other riot grrrl at school, my best friend and the first girl I'd had sex with, to enter a world of rich preppy Catholic girls. I wouldn't fit in. I wouldn't have any friends. But I was determined to focus on school. Attending an out-of-state university was my only hope for escape from a devastating household, and a college preparatory high school would get me there. I would suffer alone, accompanied only by my feminist punk ethics and the soundtracks of my favorite local bands. I would be a social pariah. A martyr for my future self.

On the first day of school, I wore my usual all black attire: flight jacket, inky tights under boy shorts, boots. My hair was super short in back with sweeping bangs that covered half my face. If I was going to sacrifice my social life, the least I could do was stay true to myself. I stood at the bottom of the stairs that lead to those looming front doors. A metal sculpture of Mary hung above the entrance, flames rising from her cupped palms. I had heartburn. I wanted to puke or pee my pants or maybe both. I started climbing, focusing on my feet as they landed on each step. I hadn't made it to the top before someone stopped me.

"Hey, are you new here?"

I looked up, expecting to find a clique of Heathers in collared shirts staring back at me. Instead, green kohl-smudged eyes met mine. I took her in. Pasty skin, violet lipstick, dyed black hair, knee high boots. Her crooked smile exposed a dimple on her right cheek.

"Yeah," I managed.

"Cool, we meet on the next block to smoke at lunch. See you then."

With that, she skipped up the last two steps and disappeared behind the heavy double doors. I stood for a minute, unsure of what had just happened. I felt an unfamiliar tickly feeling in my chest. Later, I would recognize it as hope.

By junior year I had settled in. Most of my nights were spent going to shows at La Luna, an all-ages venue in Southeast, drinking, and going to parties. I hung out with the only group of queer-leaning riot grrrls at school. Maria, the girl who'd approached me on my first day, was a year younger than me, along with Caitlin and Michelle. Mo was a sophomore, too, but she'd flunked freshman year so she was actually the same age as Amy and me. I was happier than I'd been at public school, more supported in my angst, and totally in love with Maria.

The only spawn of two geniuses, Maria exuded brilliance. Each word she used was intentional, without being strained. She had a quirky sense of humor and could be downright goofy—I loved this about her. Her frame was petite, but her mane of black hair made her look bigger. She had a bounce in her step that made her soft curls dance, and her smile was lopsided and genuine. We bonded over a love of radical feminism and queercore music. I'd written the lyrics to Bikini Kill's "For Tammy Rae" and passed it to her between classes, a punk love letter.

By prodding Amy for information, I'd learned that Maria ground her teeth at night and liked showers so hot her fair skin turned crimson. She was an unapologetic extremist. Before I knew her she had drunkenly run across a four-lane highway trying to get home. She was hit by a car and had to have her jaw wired shut for three months. She confided in me that sometimes she missed the pain.

Amy was a true badass—charismatic and engaging with a

mean streak that bordered on terrifying. She collected personal information like some people collect knick knacks. Although she had enough gossip material to bring down the Pope, she rarely used it, gleaning pleasure from the sheer power of knowing she could. She accentuated her severe hourglass shape with pegged stretch jeans and altered pearl snap shirts. In attitude and stature, her presence was undeniable.

Mo was Amy's best friend. I didn't trust her. Something about her shit-eating grin and menacing blue eyes told me she'd turn on anyone in a heartbeat. She was always doing some sketchy drugs, caught up with some gross guy. She kept her head shaved, which drew attention to her caricature-like features. I'd done acid with her once and hallucinated that her head detached from her body and floated just above her shoulders like a balloon. Since then I'd avoided looking at her for long intervals.

At one time, Caitlin and Maria had been best friends, but they'd recently started to outgrow each other. Caitlin was tall and slender and routinely sent home from school for "inappropriate dress." A natural blonde, she dyed her hair jet black. Her eyes were huge and icy blue surrounded by thick pale lashes. Her older sister was a lesbian who ran a used clothing store in San Francisco and dated Linda Perry from 4 Non Blondes. This made Caitlin one sister away from celebrity, a rock star twice removed. This would make most people automatically considered cool. But Caitlin was annoying. She was easily excited, and when she got excited she got loud. Really loud. Not only would she increase in volume, but her screechy voice would audibly split, somehow reaching multiple octaves simultaneously. Despite this obvious handicap she fronted a band called the Vagitators that played mostly in basements, and made money working as the voice for an automated customer service line.

I was closest with Michelle. She was my bro. We both came from similar class backgrounds and abusive households and we bonded over survivor issues that no one else in our friend circle could understand. Her mom was a nurse and her dad a veteran and professional junkie. Michelle was a total dude. I adored her stoner talk and constant smirk. We mostly joked around with each other and got high. Her thick wavy hair was worn dirty and parted in the middle and an endless supply of black band T-shirts and ripped jeans adorned her hulky frame.

One Friday after school we all went to Michelle's house to celebrate her sixteenth birthday. Her older asshole brother had provided the alcohol and we had all planned to sleepover. I'd been talking myself up for the party all week. I was relying on booze to give me enough false confidence to profess my love to Maria. She'd be in love with me too and then we'd make out and spend all of our time together, write manifestos and smash patriarchy with the mere existence of our hot radical queer love. I had it all planned.

Michelle's room was the size of a walk-in closet. She slept on a futon that, when folded down, left about a six-inch walkway along the wall to the door. For her party, she had set up two folding lawn chairs and a painter's stool facing the propped up futon. I took a seat next to Michelle on the more comfortable option, hoping Maria would sit next to me. Instead, she sat on the stool in the far corner.

She caught my questioning eye and looked down. "I'm little so I'll take the little stool," she giggled. "I'm taking one for the team."

Amy rolled her eyes. "Yeah, Team Fatty thanks you."

I tried to hide my disappointment. I wanted her to take one from my team.

Mo and Amy piled in next to her, sinking their beer cans

into the built-in cup holders of the lawn chairs.

That left Caitlin.

"Incoming!" she yelled crashing into me and spilling whiskey Coke down half my shirt. "Sorry!" She laughed and poured some onto her own white tank top. "Guess the wet T-shirt contest is starting early."

"Jesus, Caitlin, at least try not to be such an idiot," Mo scoffed.

I took a swig from a bottle of Jim Beam to hide my smile. I'd thought it was funny.

We toasted the birthday girl, and the whiskey bottle circled the room.

Mo had recently found out she was pregnant and took two pulls from the bottle. "I'm drinking for two!"

Five rounds later, I felt slow and hazy. The alcohol swished in my belly, soaking my crushed-out giddiness and casting it in an amber depression.

Maria had avoided talking directly to me all night. She hadn't even looked my way for more than a split second at a time.

I wanted her to see me. I wanted her to see that I was in love with her. Even one look would be proof of reciprocity.

I cracked a joke about her dad looking like Albert Einstein.

He really did.

Everyone laughed.

Maria laughed too, averting her eyes.

I stared at her, boring my eyes into her raven black hair. I would will her to look my way. If it worked for Drew Barrymore in *Firestarter*, why shouldn't it work for me?

I chanted in my head "look at me, look at me, look at me." Nothing. I was resorting to elementary school tricks, and it was pathetic.

The room was spinning and the noise of everyone talking at once crashed against my eardrums in muddled waves.

Why wouldn't she just fucking look at me?

We'd been flirting for months. My body buzzed when I was near her. She was brilliant, gorgeous, hilarious, and deep. She was in my dreams. I spent hours thinking about brushing my fingertips along her soft pale skin. I listened to Hazel's Green Eyes on the bus ride to school every morning.

I felt crazy. Had I been imagining our connection this whole time?

I looked up at her one more time. She had been staring at me.

I couldn't play this game anymore. Either she acknowledged me, and therefore her feelings for me, or I was done with it.

So, I did what any desperate, sexually frustrated homo would do in my situation.

I made out with Caitlin.

I don't know how it happened exactly. I just kinda fell into her mouth. She kissed me back like she'd been waiting for it. Her lips were soft and her tongue guided mine, clumsy from drink. Her hand crept under my shirt and caressed the underside of my breast. I couldn't tell if she was feeling me up, or correcting my wavering balance. I didn't care. I pulled my fingers through her hair, faking it through my flaccid desire.

Monday morning and I didn't want to go to school. I had barely recovered from my epic hangover and more importantly I didn't want to see Maria. Or Caitlin. I was fuzzy on the details, but I recalled enough to know I'd acted like a total jackass. I'd alienated Maria, not to mention my friends, and started something with Caitlin I had no intention of continuing.

I arrived late. It was already second period. I wandered down an empty Junior Hall to put away my bag and coat.

A folded note was taped to my locker. I opened it, hoping it wasn't from Caitlin. "Would you like to sleep over at my house this weekend?" was scrawled in a single line across the middle of the page. I recognized the small perfectly uniform letters. It was from Maria.

My heart raced and I ran to class suppressing the urge to emit a series of girlish squeals. Maria wanted me to spend the night with her. I felt validated and hopeful. She had feelings for me, she'd just been too shy or conflicted or whatever to show me. I could forgive that. I was an understanding person.

Classes flew by, my mind lost in daydreams about our future together. And about her grinding on my thigh.

At lunch I searched the crowded halls for Maria. I caught sight of her bouncy black hair as she headed out the front doors. I followed, trying to catch up. Two steps in and I stumbled on someone's foot. "Watch where you're go…" I looked up to see Caitlin. She was smiling.

"Hey, I've been looking for you," she said. "Want to grab something to eat?"

I'd been dreading this moment. She actually thought there was potential for us to hang out. I had to nip it in the bud.

"Look, what happened at the party—" I was talking quickly. "It's never going to happen again."

She opened her mouth but I continued.

"It was fun at the time but I was really drunk."

She nodded. "Yeah, totally, well I just thought…"

I cut her off. I didn't want to hear any thoughts. "We're just not on the same level," I reasoned. "You're like a little girl to me."

That seemed to hit a nerve. Her big pale eyes turned glossy and she looked away. "Yeah, whatever," she said softly. "I didn't really think it was a big deal either."

Why was she trying to act so cool about it? Her hurt look

was killing me. It would be so much easier if she just cried, confirming her feelings and giving me the satisfaction of feeling like a jerk.

"OK," I said, backing away from her. "I'll see you around." With that, I jaunted outside. But Maria was already long gone.

After school, I walked down to the Big Bang warehouse to look for clothes. I wanted a new outfit for my sleepover with Maria. I sifted through racks of used dresses, vintage lingerie, old man pants, and ratty T-shirts. After about an hour, I left with nothing but an incense headache and headed to Ozone Records to replace my Starpower tape that had melted on the dash of Amy's car. I flipped through records and perused the tapes. Nothing looked good. I was distracted. I couldn't shake the hurt look on Caitlin's face. I tried to push her from my mind. Why did I feel guilty? It's not like I'd asked her out. I didn't even like her. We were drunk. Kissing her had been a necessary test of Maria's feelings for me.

Satisfied with my weak justifications, I walked to the bus mall to catch the 56. I had avoided going home for long enough.

As I waited, Brandi, one of downtown's resident queens approached me wearing a rainbow tube top and glitter platforms. She was a regular performer at The City, the only underage gay club in town, whose catty Whitney Houston-obsessed onstage persona, Honey Miss, was merely her usual self with a bigger wig.

"Hey Cunt, I didn't see you at the club last week." She also had an endearing way of using various euphemisms for female genitalia in lieu of first names.

"Yeah, got a little too wasted." I looked down and shifted my weight. "Made out with Caitlin."

Was I so desperate for absolution that I needed to confess

to one of the town's most heartless gossips?

"Sluuuuuut!" She crooned, leaning back and posing with one hand on her hip. "Please, I know that Pussy wasn't as good as my Whitney impersonation."

"Well, it's not going to happen again," I mumbled.

"Wait, she that annoying bitch with the lezzie sister?"

Both were true.

"Girl, when she gets excited she sounds like a wounded hen runnin' from the chopping block." Brandi launched into screechy squawks, frantically flapping her elbows and dragging one foot around as if her ankle were broken. A trail of pink glitter marked a circle on the pavement. She was cracking herself up.

"It's not that bad," I said defensively. It was one thing for me to think something as a friend and another for some bitch with a cheap, synthetic weave to talk shit about the girl I'd just made out with. "She's the singer in a band," I added—as if that were any justification.

This just made Brandi laugh harder. Reviving her wounded poultry act, only this time shrieking indecipherable chicken language into a mimed microphone.

I looked around for an out. People were staring. I was sick of her.

"Oh, hey, there's Mo and Amy—Amy!" I called with a wave.

"Hey we've been looking for you," Mo yelled.

"I gotta go," I said, starting across the street.

Brandi called after me, "alright Hooch, but I better see your nasty Vagina at the Rosebud and Thorn Pageant next week!" And then louder, "and tell your friend yellow is NOT her color."

I caught up with Amy and Mo. "Thanks for saving me."

Mo shook her head. "I *know* I don't look good in this color," she said, "no one does. That's the point." Mo was wearing an ankle-length polyester dress, one of many in her collection. This one was sleeveless and a fluorescent mustard color that made your eyes spasm when you looked at it. Brandi was right, it didn't look good on her, but it was the '90s and ugly was cool. Hideous was cooler.

"Dude, you were wasted the other night." Amy looked at me, cigarette smoke slowly escaping her lips. "What was up with you and Caitlin?" Her eyes narrowed. It was her no-bullshitting face.

"Yeah, she had two buttons undone on your pants before I dragged her off of you," Mo said.

This was news to me. By that time I had slipped blissfully into the loving arms of a black out. "She was trying to get in my pants?" I asked, trying to hide my intrigue.

"Yes!" Mo made her eyes wide and hung her mouth open for effect. "She actually thought we'd let her sleep in there with you. Pathetic."

"Totally," I answered half-heartedly. I had to admit I was impressed. I admired Caitlin's boldness for putting the moves on me. "Well, don't worry," I continued. "I talked to her today."

"Good," Amy said. "This better not be going anywhere." It was a threat, but the implied consequences were unclear.

The rest of the week at school was spent awkwardly avoiding Caitlin. In all honesty, she was avoiding me too. She'd started spending lunch hour with a nerdy girl from her chemistry class who rocked long hippie skirts with green Doc Martens. I ate alone. I was sick of hanging with the crew and I was distracted with planning the details of my sleepover date with Maria. We hadn't really talked about it. I had left a note on her locker confirming my interest and she wrote one back. Saturday, 6 o'clock.

Friday I woke up early. I was too excited to sleep. One more day of school and then sweet sweet make-out time with Maria. I could hardly wait. My outfit was planned down to my underwear and I had been rehearsing all the things I would say to her. How beautiful she was. How much I loved her. How we could change the world together.

At school, I spaced out most of first period. When I headed to my locker to change out my books another note greeted me. Maria's handwriting. "Meet me at Umbra Penumbra at lunch." It was an artsy café that I routinely visited after school, mostly because other high school kids didn't go there and it was one of the only places that served chai. I was nervous, excited, and curious. I wondered what she wanted to talk to me about. I had a good feeling. Perhaps she would finally tell me she was madly in love with me.

Lunch hour and I walked down to the café where Maria was already waiting at an outside table. She was smoking as usual and her bangs were flopped down in her face. She brushed them to the side when she saw me approach.

"Thanks for meeting me," she said.

"Thanks for inviting me," I replied with a coy smile. "Want to get a drink?"

Maria ordered a regular coffee and I ordered a chai with soy milk. I paid for both and looked around for a private place to sit. The café was packed. There was something happening on stage. The audience was dead silent and everyone wore black. One guy was sporting sunglasses. I strained to see what they were looking at. In the center of the stage was a single shadeless lamp exposing a bare bulb. A thick piece of wire with a tiny papier-mâché eyeball at the end circled the light source. I didn't get it.

We sat outside.

Maria was quiet, looking into her coffee mug.

"I'm excited to hang out with you tomorrow," I tried.

"Yeah, I wanted to talk to you about that." Her tone was off. "I can't do it."

"Is it a schedule conflict?" I asked. "We could do it another time."

"No, I mean I can't hang out with you."

I was starting to panic. "Why?" I managed to choke out.

"We're just going different places."

"What are you talking about?" I was genuinely confused.

"Well," she hesitated. "It's just that, well, I'm planning on going to Harvard and I need to start thinking about my future and what that means."

I was going to be sick.

"But you're a sophomore!" I scoffed. "What does that have to do with right now?"

"We're just really different." She was still talking in ambiguities. "At this point in my life I want to have a relationship with someone who has similar long-term goals."

At this point in her life? Long-term goals? What, was she fifty? "I'm not asking you to marry me," I said, stunned. "I just wanted to hang out with you." The reality of what she was saying shook my rib cage. I could feel the hurt and anger swelling up my insides. I wasn't going to let her get away with it. "Are you telling me you don't want to make out with me because I'm poor and not Ivy League enough for you?" I was holding back tears. I didn't even want to hear her answer.

"It's not like that…"

"Wow, how amazingly classist of you," I sneered.

She didn't say a word.

"All those grand philosophical heart-to-hearts about equality and eradicating oppression were total bullshit," I continued. "Who knew underneath it all you were so fucking shallow?"

Her lip quivered. I couldn't bear to look at her. I stood and walked away as fast as I could, aimlessly heading away from her. Tears stung my cheeks in hot streams, blurring my vision. How could I have been so naïve as to think a rich girl headed to Harvard would care anything about smashing the system that promoted her privilege? That she could care about a person like me? I was angry that she had made a surface decision about our possibilities based on the class status I had inherited. Why did I always want what I couldn't have? I felt duped and heartsick. I couldn't believe I had bought her a cup of coffee.

When I finally slowed down, I was in the Park Blocks by the university. I sat down on the grass and buried my face in my jacket, letting my body give in to convulsive sobs. I didn't want to go back to class. I wanted to sink into the dirt. I never wanted to go back. But I had a mid-term fifth period. Reluctantly, I picked myself up and started towards school, wiping mascara from my ruddy cheeks.

When I arrived, fourth period was already in session. I walked to my locker, bypassing the attendance desk. After grabbing my books, I sat on the cold linoleum floor. It was quiet and I was comforted by my loneliness. A pair of the most beautiful crimson peep-toe wedge heels interrupted my pity party.

"Are you OK?" Caitlin asked. The sound of her voice surprised me. We'd been ignoring each other all week. I ran my gaze from her pumps up her tight red leather pants to her perky bra-less breasts and fixed my eyes on hers. Obviously, the nuns were sending her home for violating dress code.

"Headed home?" I asked, changing the subject.

"I don't see what the big deal is," she complained. "We're all girls, right?"

I could see her nipples right through her white T-shirt. Her hair was parted in the middle, exposing blonde roots. She'd donned two baby barrettes, one on either side, securing her bangs. A single piece of star confetti decorated the corner of one eye.

I couldn't tell if I wanted to be her, or have sex with her, or both.

"I want to leave too," I admitted, "but I have a test next period."

She gave me a sympathetic look that made me feel like a child.

"I should go," I said, picking up my books.

"Well, see you later then." She turned slowly and walked away, her heels echoing down the hall with each click clack.

I watched her, admiring her lithe body and perfect balance. She turned around, and I looked away, trying to act like I hadn't been checking out her ass.

She raised an eyebrow. "My band's playing a show tonight with Third Sex," she offered. "You should come if you want."

I looked at her and she held my gaze. I was raw and exhausted. Why couldn't I accept that I was worth pursuing? I was always running from girls who showed any interest in me. For once, I wanted to stand my ground, try something new. "I'd like that," I said.

The Empty House
sts

I met D'André when he was five. A round little boy with a million questions on his hot red face. I don't remember exactly how we met except that he was suddenly always over at the Empty House where I lived on NE 8th and Emerson.

"Is uncle Wyatt a girl or a boy?" he'd ask.

"He's a boy," we'd say. "He was born a girl, but he's really a boy."

Uncle Wyatt wore cowboy hats and ate steak and eggs for breakfast. He slept in the upstairs room next to Emilia. Down the hall in the big room was Ilka. Wyatt and Ilka had moved here from Texas and somehow I ended up at the Empty House with them. I lived in this room cut by a sloppy, half-built drywall partition.

I worked at the YMCA after school program at Alameda with all these screaming and needy kids, and then when I came home, D'André would run across the intersection of 8th and Emerson, past the crooked wood gate, under the holly tree, and up our crumbling cement stairs.

The front door was painted green, and then for no reason there was an enormous splash of red like someone kicked a paintbrush into the door.

D'André pounded on that front door incessantly. *Bam bam bam! Bam bam bam bam bam bam bam!* went D'André at 6:30 p.m., right when I got home. My nicotine patch itched on my arm. I felt tired, but I opened the door.

"Hi, Shay-ana," he'd beam. Then he'd show me something he had, like a battered kitten in a box, or candy, or a dollar, or his brother's bike. Once, he had these large plastic shoes buckled to his feet. They had big fat springs on the bottom, and he bounced awkwardly on the porch, balancing against the doorjamb.

"What are those?" Uncle Wyatt jumped off the couch. "Can I try?" He was wearing ski goggles.

D'André sat down on the floor and unbuckled the spring shoes. "Don't break 'em," he said. He sucked on a huge plastic pixie stick with green stripes. His tongue was green. We sat on the steps, D'André in his socks, watching Uncle Wyatt as he tried to bounce.

"This is so fucked up!" Wyatt yelled in his southern drawl. "They let little kids wear these'n they come home with all their ankles'n shit broke!" He tried to bounce down the sidewalk, holding the fence for support as he went.

"How are you doing today?" I asked D'André. "Have you eaten dinner yet?

"No." He shook his head, didn't stop shaking it. He just shook and shook, no, no, no, no. He opened his mouth and let some spit come out onto his lips. "Uh, uh, uh, uh," he said, in rhythm with his head moving so fast back and forth. Then he went up and down, up and down, then back to no, back and forth, back and forth. He gripped the pixie stick in his left hand. I reached out and gently took it from him.

"Your grandma makin' dinner for you?"

"No, no, no, no," he said, rocking back and forth.

"D'André, stop shaking your head."

"Why?"

"Because it's crazy."

"It feels good, though," he said, "when I stop everything looks funny." He smiled and looked at the world. All the blood was sloshed around in his head and his eyes looked all cracked out and happy.

"Come inside for some tofu and greens," I told him.

"What's tofu?" he asked, skeptical, but he followed me into the kitchen.

"You know, you've had it before."

"Oh that, I don't like it." He eyed the plate of fried tofu and kale.

I dished out some brown rice and gave him a bottle of Bragg's and jar of nutritional yeast powder. "Well, you ate the whole plate last time."

"You got any chicken?"

"No, I'm a vegetarian."

"That's right," he said, nodding slowly, and then picking up the pace. He couldn't balance the fork on its way to his mouth, and the food fell back onto his plate.

"I think you're allergic to sugar," I said, putting my hand on his back. I had only just found out there was such a thing as being allergic to sugar. I was beginning to suspect I was allergic to coffee, sugar, nicotine, alcohol, and everything else that was good.

"What's allergic?" he asked.

"It means when you eat something, it may taste good, but it hurts your body and makes you feel bad."

"I'm allergic to tofu and greens, cuz they don't taste good *and* they make me feel bad," he said, mouth full and disappointed.

The next day, D'André arrived eating a wet, red sausage the size of a huge pickle.

"D'André, what is that thing?" asked Uncle Wyatt.

"It's a Hot Mama, you can get 'em at the store for a dollar. The Man gave me a dollar, and told me to go get something to eat, so I got a Hot Mama."

"D'André," said Wyatt, "even I wouldn't eat that."

So maybe the first time D'André came into the house it was to eat some gay vegan food that was either dumpstered or stolen. He was round and happy and young, even if he was a little bit crazy—crazy in a different way than other five year olds.

Over meals in the kitchen and trying not to smoke on the front porch, I started to ask him about his life. He already knew my housemates and girlfriend. He came to punk shows in our basement, keeping his own set of earplugs on a shelf. He had a vague idea of who was trans and what that meant, and he hung out on our porch all summer long, listening to us talk.

D'André told me he lived with his grandma because his mom and dad were on drugs and they couldn't live with him. He said his dad was in Beaverton as if it was some unreachable, faraway city. He didn't know where his mom was. He said he missed her, and didn't know if she loved him. So he'd ended up living with his grandma Marion who lived in the white house with the green AstroTurf steps across the street. She had AIDS and was quickly going blind. She and D'André lived half the winter without electricity or heat until Marvin, the man who fixed cars two doors down and was raising four boys and girl on his own, fixed it, so in mid winter there was suddenly lights on over there.

Marion stood on her steps to call D'André home for the night. Sometimes she walked over and asked us to watch him for the night, if he could sleep on the couch in his sleeping bag.

"He won't be any trouble," she said. "He isn't even afraid of the dark."

Thinking of everyone fucking and drinking and cussing all through every night at the Empty House, I always said no. Maybe because I was afraid of inheriting a child at twenty-seven, and if I said yes, then Marion might feel like it was OK to die, because D'André had a home. I was filled with guilt as I watched D'André lead her down the steps back to their house saying, "It's OK Shay-ana, I ain't afraid of the dark." I closed the door to that and didn't want to think about it.

On a morning that followed another of these interactions, I heard children screaming outside. I heard Wyatt yelling D'André's name over and over from the porch, as if he were trying to get him to stop doing something. I bolted out the front door to see what was happening. It was D'André in a fight with one of the Latino boys from the next street over. There was a whole block of houses where a small Latino community lived. The children circled our block on bikes and old skateboards, and invariably one group of kids taunted the other. In this case, D'André had picked a kid off his bike and was beating him with it. He was bigger than the small boy on the ground, who lifted his arm up to block the blows. Wyatt and I got to them at the same time. Wyatt grabbed the bike, and I grabbed D'André. He screamed through the sides of his throat.

"I'm gonna kill you, I'm gonna kill you, I'm gonna kill you!" The kid lay on the ground, frozen in fear and pain. Wyatt tried to soothe him, lifting him up and pointing him in the direction of his home. A large mass of children, none older than ten, converged around us in the middle of the street. Wyatt passed the bike off to one of the boys huddled around the injured child. There were no adults except us. Everyone was silent except for D'André, screaming every single offensive and degrading term he could manufacture. His face went from brown to red. Veins bulged out of his head as he tried to tear away from me. I dragged him away from the kid on the street.

"Stop D'André, stop—" my words choked in my throat. He pulled away from me so hard I was afraid I was going to hurt him if I hung on, but even more afraid of what would happen if I let him go.

"Stop, stop, it's OK, shhh, André, shhh." I knelt down with him in front of me, pulled his arms around his body so he hugged himself while I tried to contain him. We had shuffled away from the boy to right in front of Marion's house.

And then D'André shifted from yelling at the boy to screaming at me. "Fuck you you white bitch! Let me go!"

"Shhh, André, it's OK, it's OK," and I started to not know what to do, except that I was about ready to hold him there all day if I had to. He screamed and screamed at me, calling me every single bad word I have ever heard. I didn't see where Wyatt had gone. I felt completely alone.

Finally, Marion came to her door. I don't know what she thought when she heard everything going on, unable to see beyond blurry lights. "D'André," she snapped. "You come inside here right now!" I looked up at her, not knowing what she had seen. I was afraid D'André would run for the boy again. I didn't know the boy was already turning his corner down the block with Wyatt, the bike, and about ten other kids. I was afraid Marion would think I was hurting him. My arms remained locked in place.

"It's OK," she said softly. "You can let him go now." The strength of my arms broke for him to run free up to his grandma's house. I stood up, crumpled, and started to cry. I ran to my house just as fast as D'André ran up into his. There was a group of people on the porch suddenly. My friend Ruth was there. My housemates didn't say anything. Ruth followed me into my room where I cried into my pillow for an hour, and then we got in my car and didn't come home for two days.

I walked up the steps to my house quickly, but he saw me. I don't know why I was avoiding him, like I was a kid myself. As soon as I was ten steps into my house I heard, *Bam bam bam bam bam bam*, on the door. I was alone in the house. I turned around and walked toward the door. This side of it looked like it had been painted with a brush that was dipped in cottage cheese. The door, the walls, the light switch covers, part of the door knob, and the window sills, all covered in dirty white clumps of paint. Tears welled up again and my throat closed. I didn't know what to say to him when I opened the door. He could have called me anything he wanted all day and all night if it made him feel better, but the thing that made me so sad was how much I loved somebody who could be so angry and so hurt himself that he would attack a boy with his own bike, almost killing him. His uncontrolled violence, the force with which he propelled the bike up above his head and down with all his strength on top of the child already prone in the street, crying and afraid and screaming, the way he yelled at the boy, the names he thought to call him, that he knew those names, that none of this was his fault, and none of it was D'André, but it was all D'André, all of everything bad that had happened added up to this little D'André. He was too small to be so big, too vast a place for me to see where anything began or ended. I didn't know if I opened the door that I would be big enough to hold any of him anymore.

He stood there outside, and I could feel his anxiety through the door. I turned the knob and eased it open, leaned against the jam. I looked at him, felt small, and his dry eyes suddenly went red and wet with giant splashing tears. He ducked his head down and stepped into my house, and pressed his cheek against my shirt, wrapping his arms around my waist. "I'm sorry Shay'ana," he said. "I'm sorry I hit that boy and I'm sorry I said those things to you."

"It's OK," I said, my throat closed and aching. "It's OK."

I held him.

And it was almost OK.

Lament for the Disappearing Girl
Tony Longshanks LeTigre

The other day I saw a girl in the bus shelter and for a second the hair on my arms stood on end. I thought it was Krystal. She had the same blades of spiked red hair sticking from the back of her head, and in profile I could see she wore similar round glasses—John Lennon-style, but larger. When she turned and I saw her face I saw that it wasn't her. Of course it wasn't her. It never will be her.

I should stop looking.

But how can I?

The first time you fall in love, like the first time you get high, is always the best and most transcendent. A part of you always seeks to return to it.

Ian Curtis wasn't kidding when he said love will tear you apart. If you're old and jaded, you can laugh at that line now. But only because you've forgotten what it feels like.

Krystal was my first.

1990: I was in eighth grade at Poynter Middle School, the ultimate loner boy. My mother had shipped me off from inside Mt. Rainier National Park where she worked, and where I'd lived in the enchanted isolation of preserved wilderness, to live with my aunt in her apartment in Hillsboro, Oregon, a depressing suburb of Portland. My aunt's apartment was in a complex that accepted Section 8 vouchers. Pretty much the projects. All around us were other low-income apartment complexes populated by welfare families and gangs of street kids. My aunt was an eccentric recovering alcoholic, rendered unemployable by medical conditions which included degenerative disc disease and arthritis. She spent her days either devouring library books in her bedroom (which she kept at a constant temperature of forty degrees and called "the Refrigerator Room") or watching sitcoms and country music videos on television. She chain-smoked and drank coffee from morning 'til night, and never wore more than a very short nightgown and panties, showing off her long bare legs, which were prone to bruises, scabs, and razor marks. Her glasses had thick Coke-bottle lenses and her hair was a Joplinesque mass of frizzy brown, just beginning to go gray. She had yellow teeth except one in the side top row that was brown—her "dead tooth." We played marathon games of gin rummy on the coffee table while *Full House* showed on the television, or I spent the night curled up in a sleeping bag on her bedroom floor reading comic books and asking her for definitions of words I didn't know. I loved her.

School, on the other hand, I loathed. Not exactly a unique sentiment for a junior high kid, but I was socially withdrawn to the point of total disconnection. I went days at a time saying nothing at all, made no attempt to form friendships, and lived almost entirely inside my head. To say I was depressed would probably be an understatement; it was more like a trance of total apathy, a silent protest against a world I hated. Kids my age seemed vicious and alien to me, and the closest thing I had to a friend in eighth grade was my French teacher, Mrs. Jarman. I always did my homework and participated when called on.

Most of the other students just screwed around, making fun of Mrs. Jarman's exquisite enunciation, which they took delight in mangling. A couple of evil harpies named Dawn and Michelle sat in the front row, commenting scornfully on everything and everyone. I hated those hags, but mostly I flew under their radar by staying tight inside my shell.

Dawn and Michelle had a way of talking to each other like they were the only two people in the room—but the rest of us were obviously an intended audience. I remember one day Dawn telling Michelle about two girls at a neighboring school who were lesbians. "They've got pictures of each other up in their lockers, and they walk to class together holding hands, and they're going to get *married.*"

"Oh... my... *God,*" Michelle sneered. "That is so dis*gusting!*"

"I know. It's a good thing they aren't here, because if I saw something like that, there's no way I could keep my mouth shut."

At some point early in the year, a girl I'd never seen before entered French class. During her brief stay she sat one seat behind me and to my right, a little removed; she gave the impression of being consumed by some intense inner struggle that left no room for schoolwork. She sat at her desk, head resting on her hands, looking bored to death or fidgeting with a necklace, making occasional scathing remarks that were both pointed and hilarious. I had the feeling that she was dangerous, a wolverine just daring someone to cross her. No one gave her any shit; even Dawn and Michelle spoke about her only in whispers, and that was when she wasn't around. Sometimes she would miss class entirely or come in late, smelling of cigarettes. I remember her asking me "Who pissed in your oatmeal?" in response to some mumbled comment of mine, which made me turn red and the kid behind me laugh.

One morning as Mrs. Jarman was going around the room collecting homework assignments she stopped at the weird girl's desk. "Krystal? Ou est le devoir?"

"Huh?"

"Ou est le devoir?" Madame Jarman repeated.

"I don't understand that."

"Where is your homework?"

"I didn't do it."

"Why not?"

"Because I didn't *feel* like it," Krystal snapped.

The class tittered in disbelief. Dawn and Michelle put their hands to their mouths. None of us had ever heard a student bitch-slap a teacher directly to her face before; it was a little shocking. Mrs. Jarman was silent a long moment. "See me after class," she finally said.

Krystal wasn't in French class the next day, or any day after that. There was no public explanation for her disappearance. I had no more classes with her and if nothing further had happened she wouldn't have made much of a mark on my memory. I was wrapped up in my own problems and in the fantasy world I had created to keep the desolation of reality at bay. I sat alone or at the table with the total reject kids at lunch and cared nothing for my appearance. Sometimes kids would tease me, but for the most part they left me alone, as though I was retarded and therefore not a legitimate target. I was the Invisible Boy.

As the school year continued, it became apparent that there was one person at Poynter who was not afraid, who in fact seemed *determined* to mark herself as an individual. I remained almost pathologically antisocial, but even I wasn't completely disconnected from the grapevine of gossip that connected the student body, so I remember the conversational ripple that spread through the halls the day a girl came to school with her head shaved. First she'd dyed it black, then cut it short, then shorter; now she'd gone all the way. In that time and place, in such a pressure cooker of conformity, where everyone worried about what they wore and what people would say and how to squeeze into their gender-role straitjackets, it was a radical move. Other kids did double-takes when they saw her strutting through the hall with her Chelsea-girl shave, carrying the little black box with the silver clasps that served as her purse. But it looked *good* on her; she had the right shape and size head. It was inspiring. With a sudden flash it hit me that this was Krystal, the girl who'd gotten kicked out of French class for snapping at the teacher. For a second time it seemed that she'd been thrust into my awareness, and this time I started to pay attention.

She would get teased sometimes, but it wasn't in the sadistic, mean-spirited way that the real outcasts were teased. For some reason beyond my ability to ascertain, Krystal was exempt from the peer retribution that would have greeted a lesser person taking her risks. And shaving her head was just the beginning. It was as if the internal turmoil I'd sensed brewing inside her during her brief stint in Mrs. Jarman's French class had finally hit peak capacity, resulting in these outbursts of self-expression. From this point on she never looked like anyone else at Poynter. She dressed awesomely, rarely wearing the same thing twice. Her style blended DIY punk, thrift-store, vintage, and glam. One day she would keep it real with a black long-sleeved top, cutoff blue-jean shorts and tights; the next it would be a backwards-turned cap and a pretty dress with lace in the front and scalloped layers at the hem; then black velour pants and a swanky green velvet dress jacket. She looked so much more cool and comfortable than most of the other kids, at home in her own style. It became a delight to come to school every day and catch my first glimpse of Krystal in the halls between classes, to see what eye-catching ensemble she'd put together. To this day, when I wake up in the morning, I think of Krystal and it inspires me to pick out an outfit I enjoy, one that I'll feel special in.

As ninth grade rolled on, my curiosity grew into intense interest and, finally, full-fledged obsession. Classes became just hour-long blocks of boredom between surveillance opportunities. Krystal was never hard to spot; she was a zebra among cattle. I even started keeping a "Krystal Capps Diary" in which I recorded what she wore each day and any other information I could glean about her.

Despite her aggressively individual style, Krystal was not a social pariah like me. I generally saw her in the company of at least one other person, either a gal pal like her best friend Christy Wible, or one of the skinny pretty boys she flirted with (I remember her playfully clawing at Rick Ball's chest saying "you sexy beast!"), or one of a couple of other boys who followed her around the halls, clearly snared by the same spell as I was, but more obvious about it.

A guy described those flamboyant boys who followed her as "fairies" to me once in the cafeteria. I remember the confused tone of his voice as he said it, as if he wasn't sure whether the cool thing was to be derisive or grudgingly tolerant.

Christy Wible, Krystal's bosom buddy, was another member of the Odd Girls' Club at Poynter—a strange angel with a beautiful face who always seemed relaxed and mellow. She told me once that I had "really beautiful eyes," and later, after I'd started to get weird myself and dyed my hair a different color every day with food coloring, she stopped me in the hall to say, "I really appreciate how creative you are with your hair." She had shoulder-length honey-brown hair and a weird casual-conversation vibe to her—as if people were interchangeable and it didn't really matter to whom she spoke. Still, the slightest attention paid to me by either Christy or Krystal was enough to make me high for several days. As my spying activities increased I began to notice the two together more and more. Once after school, when most everyone had gone home and the custodians were getting out the mop buckets, I caught sight of Krystal wearing a long black coat and carrying her black box, wandering the nearly empty halls. I followed her stealthily, and heard her ask a faculty member "have you seen Christy Wible? She was supposed to meet me here."

I felt bad for her missed connection and barely suppressed the urge to follow her out of the schoolyard and beyond. Did she see me? Did she know I was following her?

The ladies didn't miss each other often, though. It was common to see Christy waiting for Krystal after class, or vice versa. I wondered where they went and what they did after school. Once when I overcame my usual reserve enough to inquire about them, a guy who sat by me in geography class told me Krystal had run away and moved in with Christy. "Problems at home," the dude said, fingering quote-marks in the air.

"They're lesbian lovers," another dude said.

There was reason to wonder, especially after the Valentine's Day dance. Normally I wouldn't have attended an optional school function, but my aunt had begun to worry about my obvious lack of social life and I'd agreed to give it a shot. She drove me to the school in her battered boat of a car and dropped me off solo, around nine o'clock. The kids waiting in line before the doors opened were mostly dorks and squares and kids with lots of "school spirit." You could tell how cool the rest of the attendees were by how long after the doors opened they arrived. There were chaperones to ensure things didn't get out of hand, but even so there was a sense of anarchy that never ensued during the dull hours of academia. The gymnasium had been converted into a dance floor complete with strobe lights and a theater-sized video projection screen hanging from the rafters. At first the dance floor was empty. Kids just milled around on the sidelines. But gradually it started to warm up. I meandered from halls to gym and back again like a bumblebee, waiting for anything of interest to happen. I was hovering back near the entrance, watching people arrive, when it happened.

She walked in the door. Her hair had been slowly growing back and it was now spiked and dyed magenta. She wore a fantastic knee-length pink velour coat with buttons down the front which hugged the curvy hourglass of her body. She was with a group of people—Christy Wible, one of the "fairy" boys, and a couple other kids with skater haircuts. But I only had eyes for Krystal. I watched her go into the bathroom, come out, be playfully cornered by two of the "fairies." Back in the gymnasium, the dance floor had begun to rock. I watched with awe as my peers cast off their inhibitions and gave themselves over to the fun. It seemed to me that everyone must be dancing to show off for someone else; but I had no one to show off for. I stood off to the side near the bleachers and watched. Christy and Krystal made their way right into the center of the action. A hot song came on—EMF's "Unbelievable" maybe? Or was it "Bust a Move?"—and the two hot ladies were rocking the floor, writhing to the music, up against each other, oblivious to everyone else. I was shocked by their abandon, but no one else seemed to notice. Watching them in that moment I felt an intense surge of contradictory emotions: elation and infinite sadness. Elation, because watching Krystal in her glory, lit up/ silhouetted in the strobe light against the writhing mass of bodies, filled me with awe. She was coolness incarnate. And sadness because I would never be that cool.

Krystal seemed oddly exempt from the attendance strictures that bound most students, and she'd sometimes come in halfway through the day, or not at all, without any apparent consequences, as if she had some sort of arrangement with the administration. One morning as I moved with the rest of the herd in through the front doors of the school, I was fascinated to see Krystal standing just inside the entryway chatting animatedly with the vice principal, he in his suit and slicked hair, she with red spikes and green eye shadow, looking ready for a wild party at eight in the morning. I could only imagine what had sparked such an unlikely conversation.

About halfway through the year I actually made a friend, a half-Mexican girl named Aida whose father was supposedly connected to the Mexican mafia. Aida's outsider perspective made her sympathetic to me and we started talking in a class, and eventually started hanging out outside of school. "You remind me of a friend I had back in Mexico City," she told me. "He wasn't interested in girls either."

I talked to Aida about my obsession with Krystal and tapped her for knowledge. She rewarded me with little nuggets of information. She'd been at a party recently where Krystal was in attendance, and said Krystal bragged about doing cocaine—"I get straight A's because I do coke, and the day I get an F is the day I stop!"—and about her father giving her three packs of cigarettes as a birthday present. "She told me she's been smoking since she was *nine,*" Aida said.

My recovering-alcoholic aunt went to AA meetings sporadically, and she was always talking to me about the AA philosophy, proselytizing it the way pious people do with religion, and pointing out defects in my character that she thought might be early signs of alcoholism, despite the fact that I'd never so much as sipped a wine cooler. Every so often she'd urge me to try out a meeting of ACOA, the Adult Children of Alcoholics, saying it would be good for me. I never gave the issue much thought until one day when she mentioned that she'd been talking to someone from one of the ACOA meetings and that she happened to know Krystal, *my Krystal*, attended from time to time.

"How did you find that out?" I asked, suddenly very intrigued indeed.

"Well, I was telling her about you, and how much of an *individual* you are, and she said, 'We have some really interesting kids who come to the meetings,' and she described this girl and I said 'I know who that is! Is her name Krystal?' and she said 'Yes.'"

One afternoon as I unlocked my bike to ride home, Krystal happened to be standing nearby talking to Rick Ball. I'd just started dying my hair with food coloring and it was bright Kool-Aid red.

"Why did you do that?" Krystal asked me pointedly.

I shrugged, cool as I could. "Why not?"

"Because it looks really *bad.*"

"Leave him alone," Rick laughed, "he just wants to be you."

Another evening as I was riding in my aunt's car we passed Krystal walking down a small side street. It was a scary part of town, the *really* bad apartments, the sun was on its way down, and she was alone, carrying her little black box. Where was she going?

"Should we offer her a ride?" my aunt asked.

"No!" I cried. *Was she crazy?* Our car was a piece of junk, my aunt was gonzo, and I was a dork. I could just imagine pulling up beside Krystal, offering her a ride and having her turn it down. I would rather have gnawed off my arm.

Then there was the day Krystal picked up a stray cat during lunch hour and brought it into the school building with her. I had career guidance class after lunch and was sitting in the hallway talking with a girl named Theresa who ended up as my "wife"—it was a class activity where we all split into our assigned pairs to discuss our career goals and "marriage" plans, and the two of us had ended up out in the hall. Suddenly there was Krystal, walking towards us with the cat, and accosting Theresa, who obviously knew her. She glanced only briefly at me, not asking my name, but let both of us pet the cat, which was wild-eyed and scruffy. Then she held the cat up with its legs spread and asked us whether it was a boy or girl.

"Krystal!" Theresa yelled, virulently looking away.

Krystal's wicked laughter trailed after her as she glided on down the hall.

"She's kind of an *out-there* girl," I baited Theresa, having identified her as a potential source of information.

"Yeah," Theresa replied, "but I wouldn't tell her that or she'll kick your ass."

Ninth grade ended and release from the hormonal prison of middle school came as a relief, but my obsession with Krystal would remain unfed for three months. When September came my stress levels were through the roof. Glencoe was much bigger than Poynter, intimidating for any freshman, let alone a quirky social hermit. On the first morning, I paced anxiously outside the building before the doors opened, hopping like a frog in search of a lily pad.

My spirits got a big boost when I caught sight of two figures strutting like peacocks through the courtyard.

They were both dressed as sort of New Wave vamps, one with carrot-orange and the other with blue-black hair, ratted and sprayed almost into beehives. They both had on lipstick in unusual colors—lime green and eggplant purple—and outfits of colorful blouses and skirts over lacy leggings. The girl with the orange hair, I found out later, was Rachel Smith. Her companion was none other than Krystal Capps. As I watched the two of them sail through the courtyard and into the school building, my spirits went up like a kite. Maybe Glencoe wouldn't be so bad after all.

Compared to Poynter, it wasn't. I had a few friends by now, including a girl named Kinsey who lived with her single mom. She was a geek and an outsider like me, but with a certain pride and self-reliance that I found familiar and likable. We both held ourselves with a certain dignity even though we were pariahs, as if not having friends was a choice. At lunch Kinsey and I and a couple other misfits sat outside on the grass or near the theater building on the other side of campus watching the cool queer people hanging out in their pod. I felt jealous, wanting to be one of them.

At Poynter, Krystal had seemed boldly original and unique, but at Glencoe she had competition. There was a dyke named Jackie Waldrop who was dating a beautiful cheerleader named Heather, and the two of them held hands and stared into each other's eyes in the hallways. Jackie had charisma; she was loud and funny and extroverted. She didn't seem to have any issues with her sexuality or her genderqueer-ness, and thought nothing of coming to school in shorts with her hairy legs on full display. There was also a boy who wore skirts and dresses to school. It was encouraging to see people like them not only surviving in the danger zone of high school but claiming their place as some of the coolest people. Peripheral members of this circle included badass babes like Tanya Golden, who usually wore a black leather jacket and boots to school, and Rachel Smith, the lipstick lesbian I'd seen Krystal arrive with on the first day. There was also a Krystal wannabe who dressed in much the same style and carried a similar black box everywhere she went, but she lacked her prototype's allure and personality.

One of the best days of my freshman year at Glencoe was the day Krystal came and sat with me and my friends at lunch. This was the closest I'd ever get to an honest one-on-one conversation. Three or four of us had left the herd to eat our lunch by the theater building. Sometimes we ate inside the theater, which was my favorite—the rich velvet curtains drawn over the stage and the vast dark quietude of the empty auditorium. But when it was nice out or the theater was locked or in use we'd settle for the sheltered concrete walkway outside the theater. And so it was on the day Krystal joined us.

She came around the corner wrapped in a blanket she'd worn to school that day over her clothes, carrying her lunch, Rachel by her side. The two of them sat down against the wall at the far end of the walkway. The walkway had nice acoustics and I heard Krystal tell Rachel about dying her hair the night before (it was purple now and getting long). She bragged about having "twenty-nine days of sobriety" and enthused about an upcoming Red Hot Chili Peppers concert with a sort of manic glee.

After a few minutes, Rachel had to leave and Krystal was alone, yards away from me and my geek corps. Solitude didn't seem to suit her and she came over to us asking "how are you people doing?" I sat starstruck as she took her seat among us and proceeded to lead the conversation.

She no longer seemed fierce and formidable as she had at Poynter; for the first time she actually seemed like someone I could approach. She was articulate and carried the conversation from tangent to tangent in an ADD sort of way, until we found her telling us about a Winter Solstice party she'd recently attended where "Rachel and I kissed beneath the mistletoe and everyone else backed away, like, 'we're not gay!'" The homophobic reaction of the other kids seemed to tickle her pink, but there was disdain beneath the laughter. The attitude embodied by her words—that queerness, far from being taboo, was actually a subversive form of cool—flew so bluntly in the face of the institutionalized homophobia I was used to that it qualified as an epiphany. *Queer could be cool.*

Not too long after the day Krystal sat with us at lunch, I was standing alone at the bus stop after school when she walked by. She had a serene look, waved at me and smiled—a warm and genuine smile. I went home and gushed to my aunt that I might actually be close to making *friends* with the mythical Krystal Capps. But it was the last time I would ever see her.

The next week marked the halfway point of the year and Krystal brusquely disappeared. Kinsey and I finally summoned the courage to ask Rachel and we learned that Krystal had "gone into home studies." Rachel seemed sour on the subject and wouldn't say more. The news surprised me. Despite Krystal's obvious shortcomings in the attendance department and lack of concentration on schoolwork, she seemed a social creature who enjoyed interacting with her peers as much as I dreaded it. It didn't seem fair that she vanished just when I felt like there might be a possibility of actually speaking with her. It didn't make sense. But nothing much did.

After my freshman year my aunt decided to move back to Minnesota, so I finished high school in a small town up north—birthplace of Judy Garland. Of the few friends I'd made in Hillsboro, I actually managed to keep in touch with Kinsey. We sustained our friendship with handwritten letters, email, and occasional phone calls. After I finished my freshman year of college in 1996, I moved to Portland to share an apartment with her. Shortly after I settled in, Kinsey said it: "Did you hear about Krystal Capps?"

I froze. "No. What about her?"

Kinsey hesitated. "She died."

I couldn't process the words. The weirdest chill went through me. I'd hardly have been more spooked if Kinsey had told me that I myself had died over the course of the summer and was visiting her now in spectral form. I listened in a numb trance as Kinsey explained the details. She'd seen it on the news just a week before: A major apartment fire in Beaverton had claimed the lives of Krystal, her fiancé Benjamin, and their sixteen-month-old daughter, Ivy. They'd been living in the Tartan West Apartments in Beaverton, one of those awful sprawling Section 8-type complexes like the one I'd lived in with my aunt. The cause of the fire turned out to be a man living below them who had shoveled ashes from a barbecue into a paper bag and left them on his porch. By 4 a.m. the ashes, not entirely cold when bagged, had reignited and started a fire that entered the apartment above through its open sliding-glass door. Krystal and Benjamin and Ivy had died of smoke inhalation, not burns. I wondered if they'd even woken up.

"The news report said their smoke alarm was disabled," Kinsey added, accentuating the tragedy. "Otherwise they probably would have made it."

"I can't believe it," I fumbled to make sense of it. "I can't believe she's actually *gone.*"

"She always seemed really lost to me," I heard Kinsey say.

I could only shake my head, and think back to the last time I'd seen her—that last day at Glencoe, waiting for the bus when she walked by. If only I could go back in time and replay that moment. Take her aside and give voice to all the things I'd felt and never said. I wish I'd said: "Krystal, there's something I've wanted to tell you since last year at Poynter, and it's now or never. Once in a while you meet someone who makes you feel you were half asleep before you met them. To me you are one of those rare people. You are the most fascinating, incandescent person in this entire school, and more. I feel there's a bond between us in some weird way even though I don't know you. I've spent days watching you move through the halls. In a hallway packed with people you are the only one there. You have this aura to you; I can see it even if other people can't. I've tried to imagine what your life must be like when you go home at night, how you got to be the person you are. Since I'm never going to see you again after this moment, I have to say it now. You showed me who I am at a time when I desperately needed it. You gave me courage that I will carry with me forever from now on. I was asleep before I met you, and now I am awake."

But of course people don't really talk like that.

Wait, that can't be the end. That's too depressing. There's an earlier moment. We'll end with that. It came halfway through our last year at Poynter, on January 15, 1991, the day the first George Bush declared war on Iraq. I don't know if I can make you feel what I felt that day, but I have to try.

Imagine, first of all, that you're fifteen years old. Everything that happens has about seven times the impact it would have on a normal, hormonally balanced, sane adult person. In that state, a moment that might seem like nothing to someone else can be life-changing.

Nothing much happened in the moment I'm about to describe—except everything.

I had detention. I wasn't the acting-out, teacher-insulting type. I'd been written up for skipping class or being tardy. Come noon—the designated detention time—I sat in the choir room where detention was held, along with a motley crew of class-cutters, delinquents, and ruffians. On some level I think I was a little proud. It meant I was a little *bad,* and badness in middle school is a badge of pride. But who was I kidding? I was a *freak*. Sitting in that silent, tense room, I was a wreck. I fidgeted in my chair and barely took my eyes off the clock, mentally pleading with it to fast-forward. I felt that everyone was staring at me and their looks were not friendly. They saw into me, all my nervousness and fragility; they hated the awkward reject within all of them I so purely reflected. I was a block of cheese in a world of cheese-graters.

All that day rumors had been circulating about a walkout planned for the lunch hour. The morning classes had been fraught with an unspoken tension, and I'd been on the edge of my seat, longing for the moment when the clock struck the appointed hour and everyone rose from their seats to silently march and merge into the halls in graceful protest. But here it was lunchtime and nothing had happened. The call to drop arms had not come. No one, it seemed, really cared.

Then suddenly, out of nowhere, I heard a female voice singing a line from "Imagine" in a sweet, alto voice: *Imagine all the people, living life in peace...*

Heads in the room turned and people shifted in their seats. The voice drew nearer and louder and the doors of the room opened and in they strode, side by side, two girls. I recognized Christy Wible, the singer, right away, but it took me a moment to identify her companion, due to her odd get-up. She wore boots painted maroon, a beautiful blue dress with a jacket sort of stitched onto and over it on top, and a blue cap turned backwards. Her face was painted white, like a mime—or a ghost. It was Krystal Capps. The sight of her filled me with something inexpressible and tremendous. It suddenly struck me that she was very beautiful, and how strange it was that I'd never noticed that before. There she was, weird like me, but not afraid.

The girls walked to the desk and Christy spoke. She gave

both their names to the lady at the detention desk; explained that she and Krystal were assigned detention but had been granted permission by Mrs. Garcia to spend the time in her room making up a test. The detention lady made them sign out on a roll sheet. I noticed Krystal didn't speak; perhaps a vow of silence was part of her protest against the unjustified war. Christy signed first, then Krystal stepped up to sign. Christy swayed gently from side to side and continued to sing a cappella: *You may say I'm a dreamer, but I'm not the only one...*

It happened so quickly, and then the two of them were strolling back out the door, Christy's angelic voice trailing away. I caught a last glimpse of Krystal's skirt swirling over her boots before she disappeared through the door. And then she was gone.

Straight and tall I sat up in my chair, for the first time all day, maybe for the first time all *year,* no longer afraid. I looked at the clock hovering above the silent classroom and saw that freedom was only five minutes away.

Ghost Bikes
Kathleen Bryson

The biggest bicycle in the world, Big Red, a bicycle towering over the tallest building downtown, spraypainted with blood and locked up next to the world's biggest stop sign. The bike in my head.

The ghost bikes keep whizzing by, and hey, there's another one, out of the corner of my eye as I ride the bus, when I'm in a car, when I'm cycling myself. There are ghost bikes on every corner, makeshift memorials with a bike U-locked to a traffic sign, bikes spraypainted white to commemorate recent fatalities. There have been a lot of fatal bike-car accidents in Portland recently. I once read in a children's book that if the first spring butterfly you saw was white, it would mean the summer would be very, very sad, but I'm pretty sure the first bike I've seen this spring is my own bright blue Nishiki, the one I ride to work each morning. A big bright blue butterfly, so fuck off, universe. It's all fine.

Today, a Saturday, Winston and I are pedestrians, walking out for coffee, and we pass by a funereal group of kids locking a bike to a steel post, think that's pretty sad, and keep on walking. But it's the second ghost bike of the day, the one across from the café now, that really gets to me.

I learned to ride a two-wheeler when I was five, much further north up in the Alaska I'd grown up in (different and the same than the Alaska that exists these days). I've been in the Lower 48 for years now, but I still remember the catch of the day, those big glitzy salmon and the smoke smell to the air, the ripe insect perfume you get when you hike in the woods. Forest Park is beautiful here in this city, but it doesn't hold a candle to real wilderness. It's ersatz wilderness, your default, what you get enough of in order to cope. Holding a candle. Christ, back in the '90s I held so many candles at so many December 1st vigils I lost the taste for it, and barely remember to wear a red ribbon these days when the season rolls round, and you'd think I, of all people, ought to remember that.

I smile at Winston across the table.

Winston winks back. "You want the arts section?" He hands over half of the *New York Times*.

Last night Winston answered the phone, chatted a bit, and then called me to the receiver to speak to my Alaskan nieces, who were begging my knowledge about an art contest they were having about tidal waves and the 1964 earthquake. (My brother felt I was uniquely qualified to weigh in on artsy matters by mere benefit of my gayness). It seems a little sick to me, capitalizing on a tragedy that's still remembered by people living, but black humor gets humans through a lot, and you'd think I, of all people, ought to remember that.

When I think of Alaska at all, it's an old bicycle of the past—the greenness, the freshness of it, but also the pain of being gay on the high school basketball team—sleeping in tents while the loons call sleekly, the volcano across the bay, the puffy snows of yesteryear that I stomped and sunk through as a kid in moonboots, the spring of senior year when Dennis Makkinen and I sucked each other off out in the woods, a picnic tablecloth spread under us so the cranberry bushes wouldn't poke up too much. I remember once looking up at the sky, and thinking that it could never get better than this. But it did. And it didn't. Dennis Makkinen faded into neverwhere again—where was he now?—and he was followed by other guys, and even a few girls, and then there had been my one true love, Craig, down in Seattle, and then another true love, Winston, here in Portland, which surprises me as much as love's ability to repeat and multiply. I had thought that was it, after Craig no more, my one-time shot, but I was wrong.

I accept the newspaper graciously. Times have changed and the *Times* has changed. Wedding announcements now, men marrying men in posed pictures. I think of Craig and me back before we both got sick, hating the very concept of marriage; you'd plaster a bright orange Queer Nation sticker over your mouth before you got a proposal out, or else your boyfriend would do it for you. Back then you'd see gay men in the obituaries instead, young men in their twenties, thirties, forties, with closeted phrases like "long-time companion," "dear friend," and often no companion mentioned at all, just an immediate family, as if a thirty-four-year-old man like Craig could exist in a vacuum that only included parents and siblings, no friends, no lovers. It was the ultimate lie.

Right there in front of us, mid-distance from Stumptown Coffee where Winston and I sit outside, that second ghost bike, pale in the sunlight, an up-bellied fish. It seems an organized jumble of bones, like a skeleton, and I reckon that's how it's supposed to seem. Except usually you don't show your bones on the outside. Skeletons are private, the ultimate skeleton-in-a-closet cases. Forced to react to death, forced to see its dinosaur bones—ossified handlebars, seat, wheels—well, like many things in polite society, it's not done. But look—it *has* been done; someone is doing it. If you want to ride, don't ride the white pony. That song was playing the summer with Dennis, long time ago.

I smile at Winston; think of our four happy years together so far, and I remember bright bumper stickers and angry red hand-printed T-shirts, where silence equaled death, but so did many other things. I think of Craig when I was in hospice, knowing he'd be next, touching his hand, and then it didn't happen that way. I get the reprieve and Craig doesn't, combination therapy makes it even better, tough luck, lover. You were a good, good guy.

The ghost bikes of Portland on every corner, white as sin, are more effective than your average tombstone. Graveyards are consigned to a different part of town. Out of sight, for the most part. The bikes usher death straight into mundane life, out of the cemeteries and into the neighborhoods, forcing you to see that death happens here, right here. Someone died here. You don't think about all the places that death takes place, usually. You try not to.

I gave my nieces a few pointers last night and then had an awkward conversation with my brother, who at least this time remembered to ask after Winston. He's learned; we've all learned. People change and times change and the *Times* changes and it all comes round again, doesn't it, Carly Simon?

I should start up an AIDS contest down here, that would stir things up in an old-fashioned, '90s way—how had the '90s already become ancient history?—too fast—it would be very ACT-UP of me, everything in capital letters; you had to fight for that back then, you had to fight for AIDS instead of Aids; you had to fight to make them pay attention.

These days it's like diabetes, my doctor says, there's a good chance I'll live out my natural life span, and I'm not the only one who vaguely wears a red ribbon on December 1st. The disease no ghost, still here, but no one talks about it. People still dying of it, people still afraid of it, people still contracting it, but nothing you can spraypaint red and lock to a stop sign on a corner.

"The wireless is out," Winston comments, Winston who is surfing on his laptop across from me and sipping an iced chai. "I bet it'll kick back in soon, though." Winston is negative but Winston is always positive. I love Winston, all my soul.

Back in Alaska, even these days, it's still all fag fag fag and AIDS kills gay people and gay people spread it, but at least it's still in capital letters. At least there isn't a contest and people making jokes like it's *Buffy* or Halloween or Count Dracula, real blood faded into fake vampire blood through the centuries. *Oh, Craig.*

As we walked past it earlier in the morning, the ghost bike, the memorial one, I briefly saw the ritual itself, young hipsters carrying bouquets and painting the bike. They were all laughing and smiling, and this seemed like the kind of funeral I'd have liked to have gone to myself. Craig's had been stressful, his parents grieving and homophobic, a terrible combination but not therapy.

I blink in the sun; sip my coffee. The sunshine is so bright it saps my energy. I look at the pale bike opposite, squint. Craig liked biking; we'd gone a lot before we both got sick. Now I'm finance litigation, and life is good in our Craftsman, dinner parties on weekends with friends, all the anger sucked out because it feels so good these days. I look across at Winston, who scowls at his crossword puzzle. It's cute the way he never asks for help. Craig always asked for help.

A butterfly wings past me, a green one. All the bicycles of your past—your hometowns, your loves, you can hide them or you can see them, but it doesn't mean they're not there, like a virus ticking its way down inside your skin, controlled or not.

I'm going to have sort out the contract on Tuesday. If that idiot new-hire in accounting doesn't get her shit worked out, our whole office is in for a nasty surprise come Christmas-bonus time. On the other hand, she brought in bagels with cream cheese last week. My heart eases towards Candy-Lee of Accounting.

"Do you want to grill tonight?" Winston asks, his hand hot on my hand. "I bought Portobellos. They'd be nice with some beer."

"Sounds great," I say and smile.

I stare out at the cycle frame, bleached out even whiter in the light. I shut my eyes and the bike is there, glowing in negative radiation like when you stare at the sun, and then I open them again to see the green of the trees, spring living green, just like Alaska, and I hear the birds tweeting over the clatter of the coffeehouse.

It's Craig on a bicycle, painted as white as snow, with streamers in the wheels like from some long-ago, small-town Fourth of July parade. He's wheeling toward me, waving, but there's no sound coming out of his mouth. The streamers spin, white skeins in the wheels. He looks free and he looks happy. White is not the absence but the combination of all colors, and here Craig is, a vapor, a wind, a white cloud, and I blink and then Craig is also pearly blue and violet and grass and garnet all at once, cinnamon-orange and saffron, the spectrum glows. Craig's in his early forties, too, like he kept on living instead of freezing in time like a photograph, and he's grinning with that fresh smile he used to have back in '89 when we were first dating, the heartbreaker smile. We used to hold hands all the time back then, in public or not, we didn't give a fuck, we were as young as spring. The bicycle is burning with color, the party-time streamers move from white to rainbows and back to dove-white again. His memorial is steady but someone with the keys has unlocked the bike, and Craig is riding free. He takes both hands off the handlebars, the showoff.

I watch until the bicycle rounds the corner, and then turn my attention back to my coffee, which tastes rather lovely as well, and I watch Winston out of the corner of my eye.

MIGRATIONS

Juliet Takes a Breath
Gabrielle Rivera

You're going where?" my mother asked. It was more a statement of disbelief than an actual question.

"Portland. I'm going to Portland, Oregon, for my internship requirement."

"Well, what are you going to do out there in Portland, Oregon, so far away on the other side of the country? It *is* on the other side, right?"

"Yes, Ma, and I already told you I'm going to be Harlow Brisbane's research assistant. She's the woman who wrote *Raging Flower: Empowering Your Pussy by Empowering Your Mind.*" I held my mother's gaze, watched the wheels in her brain click back.

"*Ohh*, the vagina book lady. Ay, Nena, you know I tried to read that thing but I had to stop bringing it on the bus with me to work. People were staring." She turned her attention to the pot of *arroz con gandules* on the stove.

"I mean, you know, I liked what I was able to read, but I just can't read a book that has the P word on it in public." She turned the rice with her large metal spoon and steam rose up.

"I get it, Ma, but we're in the house now and I think you can say pussy in your own home." I leaned against the marble island in our kitchen, watching her cook, savoring the smells.

She turned to me, that metal spoon still in her hand. "The P word is a nasty word that men use to be vulgar. So if you're going to refer to it or even say it in my house, it's the P word." She gestured with her spoon. "I prefer to call it a flower."

"Fine. No callin' it a pussy when it's a flower," I laughed. "Besides, we're totally off topic, Ma. I believe we were discussing my internship."

"Right, right. So you're going to help the vagina lady do research." She put the lid back on the pot and looked at me.

"Yeah, she's trying to write her fourth book and it's turning into quite the daunting task. We haven't exactly defined my role in her creative madness, but I'm sure I'll become well acquainted with Portland's public library."

Ma placed cloves of garlic in front of me, wordlessly instructing me to get to smashing. "Well, Nena, whatever you wanna do. You're always doing some crazy thing or another anyway. At least this one is for school. As long as you get the credits you need, your father and I support you. Even if you're going all the way to Utah."

"Oregon."

"Whatever place across the country it is you're headed. It'll be fine. You're so adventurous, Juliet. You didn't get that from me. That's from your father's side of the family, I'm sure of it." And then she changed the subject.

I didn't mind. I loved being in the kitchen with Ma, sharing bits of my life as we cooked. If we didn't cook together, how would I ever get to know her? And when that steaming plate of food was placed in front of me, would it really matter that she'd just said I was crazy like my dad's family for the nine billionth time? Not at all.

Dinner was amazing. I even got my father's blessing for my adventure.

"Oh my God! You're really going to work with Harlow Brisbane?!" My girlfriend, Laney, squealed into the phone.

"Yeah, babe, the one and only." I stretched out on my bed, resting my cell phone between my ear and the pillow. "But you know all of this already, Laney. You've been with me every step of the way. From my first phone call with Harlow to my meeting with Professor O'Donald to approve it as an internship. How can you still be surprised, woman?" I reached for the remote on my nightstand.

"First of all, don't call me woman." She was already getting feisty. How can one girl be so seriously literal all the time?

"I know, babe, jeez. I'm just saying. How come I can call a squirrel a squirrel but I can't call my woman a woman?" It was so much fun to bust Laney's chops. I still can't figure out how such an intelligent girl always took my bait.

"Oh, here we go with your machisma bullshit. You just don't get it, do you? I'm not your possession. Remove the *my* from your sentence." She's dead serious, but all I hear is: *Blah dee blah bark blah possession bo beep.*

"And furthermore," she's saying.

Oh God, there's more.

"Calling me *woman* denies me an identity and a voice, which is what men have been doing to women since the beginning of time. I'm so glad you're going to Portland, Juliet. Harlow is really going to have fun molding you into a woman who respects women."

I could feel the smug grin creep across her face.

I yawned into the phone. "I never said I didn't respect women. I just don't respect overly sensitive borderline crazy liberal feminists from Westchester county." I bit my tongue to keep from laughing.

Shit, is that steam coming from the phone?

What I hear next is a cross between a harrumph, a growl, and a girly-sounding squeal of disgust. "Juliet, you are impossible, incorrigible, and completely impervious to everything I say."

"But I love you, girl, and you love me. So what's the big fucking deal? You still picking me up from the train tomorrow?"

"Yeah, we'll do lunch in Hartsdale and then go to the galleria so you can buy whatever last minute things you need for your trip." I could tell that I'd gotten her to smile, just a little bit.

"Awesome. I'll call you tomorrow and you can school me on some more of whatever it was you were trying to say, babe." I flicked through the TV channels, barely registering what was on the screen.

"OK, babe. I'm super excited for you," she gushed.

"Word, babe." I clicked my phone shut and lay there thinking, the television on mute. Laney was just too focused sometimes, you know? The world and the people in it are way bigger than any one-sided rhetoric. No matter how aware or informed someone is, touting beliefs as if they're the only one true way is condescending and self-righteous. On top of that, it's annoying. It leaves people like me stuck in between. Sometimes I feel like I'm sitting in the stands, drinking beer and throwing popcorn at the conservative zealots and overbearing liberals.

But I do love me some Harlow Brisbane. She tells people to fuck off with their judgments and shows no fear of expressing anything she thinks or feels. Yeah, freeing the poon tang from white male oppressive westernized misogynistic and racist barriers is awesome, but you don't have to do it by writing a thesis paper or having weekly meetings with the feminism choir. Sometimes you can do it by just being you. That's what Harlow Brisbane says. And that's why I'm hauling my ass all the way to Portland, Oregon, to be her research assistant.

Besides, the shit I talk to Laney is just a buffer system I use when I feel like I'm being patronized. It's my way of saying: Bitch, we go to the same college and take the same women's studies classes and you think you have to educate me? Get out of my face with that mess. I say live and let. Then when you see someone really being mistreated, step up. Don't just talk shit in your elitist little circle and think you're being progressive. You have to push yourself outside your comfort zone. That's what Harlow is urging us to do and that's what I feel like I'm doing. Harlow has the balls that have yet to drop on me and that is why I'm going to Portland. It's not just a fucking internship. This whole trip is going to change my life.

7:19 a.m. My alarm clock goes off and I spring up with a start. Jeezus! What's today? What the fuck? I went shopping with Laney on Saturday and had some relatively decent good-bye sex. Sunday night I had dinner with the family at the Wild Tortilla. But now I'm flying to Harlow. Today! What the fuck is a Puerto Rican girl from the Bronx doing flying out to Portland, Oregon? I pull the covers over my head.

As I start to drift back to sleep, Ma knocks on the door.

"Nena, I'm making breakfast. Eggs sunny side up with bacon and coffee. Come. Eat."

"Ma, can I have mine scrambled instead? You know I think runny eggs are gross." I enjoy the fact that at age twenty, I can still be making the same breakfast request I'd been making since I was eight.

"Of course, Nena, you got it. Get out of bed and come down." I hear her footsteps as she walks away. "My baby's going to Idaho."

"Oregon," I mumble.

The rest of the morning is a blur of breakfast, luggage, and tight hugs goodbye.

Bye Ma.

Bye Dad

Bye Bro.

Bye Laney.

You can't fly straight to Portland from New York, so Hello, Vegas. Peace out, Vegas.

Shit, now it's nighttime and I'm stepping off a plane in a state that I've never once even as a joke wanted to set foot in. Am I crazy? Worry kicks in like a drunken stepfather. Harlow sounded like a super-intelligent guru on the phone, but part of me suspects that her attention was focused on social and political ideas. Real life, mundane tasks, or appointments— like remembering to pick up her dry cleaning or a strange kid at the airport—might just slip her mind.

Oh my God, I'm going to be abandoned by Harlow at the airport. Don't cry yet, dumbass, get your luggage first.

Geared up with two bags and a carryon, I head for the nearest exit. As I'm chilling, heading down the escalator, I see her. I know it's her and from the moment our eyes meet, she knows it's me, too.

Her bright red hair is what I notice first. Then her clear and shocking blue eyes. A red head with big blue eyes and dimples on a chick normally turns me into the charm bandit, but there's something off about her. Her face is a little asymmetrical and one of her eyes is slightly bigger than the other. And Harlow's got one of those gazes where you know she's looking at you, but you wonder if she's actually seeing you as a flesh and blood person. Perhaps all she sees are particles of extra life in the way of her view of existence. She is beautiful in a way that I've never experienced. I don't want to fuck her, but I can't imagine not being in her presence.

And all this before I even reach the bottom of the escalator.

"Ahh, my Julieta, you're as beautiful as I imagined." Harlow wraps me in a full body hug. "Oh and wow, your aura smells so fresh." She lifts the duffel bag off my shoulder and picks up her pace as she leads me to the exit.

"Thank Goddess about your aura, Miss Julieta, because quite honestly, I would have sent you back on the next flight to New York if your aura had a foul aroma." Harlow nods seriously. She doesn't laugh, so neither do I. For the first time in my life, I'm elated that I have a great smelling aura. But I wonder just how stable the next few months in Portland are going to be.

The second I scope Harlowe's car—a Pepto-Bismol-pink pick-up truck with hand-painted daisies on both sides—I feel in my core just how incredibly far from the Bronx I really am. As we drive away from the airport, my whole body feels different. I am supremely alert, all of my senses razor sharp. It must be the air. I can taste its crispness. I feel my lungs widen with each breath. Asthma has plagued my little Spanish ass since birth. The Bronx has the highest asthma rate in New York. You can taste the sour stench of exhaust and garbage with every inhalation. But now I feel completely different. I feel connected to this place already. Its air fills me. This glorious Portland air—one breath at a time. My posture relaxes. Even my thoughts feel loftier. The three inhalers I've packed and the double stash of Benadryl in my duffel bag might just stay there all summer. I let my thoughts drift as I count my breaths.

"Your mind is blank, Julieta," Harlow says cryptically. "Tell me why that is." She grabs a hand-rolled cigarette from the dashboard and lights it. She inhales deeply and I can hear the paper burn.

"I'm just breathing, lady. Never felt air like this inside of me." I wonder if the air is turning me into a hippie as we drive.

"In order to truly fucking *get* the enormity of our situation—of you here with me—I encourage you to keep your body as pure as the air you are breathing." Harlow speaks like a prophet as she puffs on her rollie. "There will be no meat in my fridge. I cannot allow the remains of once massive and incredible creatures rotting in any part of my home and especially not where I keep what nourishes me."

I nod. I have prepared myself for this. College had me feeling like I was intellectually superior to most everyone else with the exception of Nobel Prize winners. But I've left all that bullshit in the Bronx. I left my cocky, loud mouth, know-it-all swagger on the corner and didn't look back.

I knew that this place, this Portland with Harlow, would be an entirely new space to exist in. I had to be ready. I wanted to absorb everything and in order to do that I knew I had to alter the way I interacted with the world. So I shut my mouth and listen.

When Harlow tells me to avoid dairy, I hear: *Let your body function without antibiotics injected into enslaved animals.*

When she encourages me to read *A People's History of the United States*, I hear: *My dearest Julieta, please study the many sides of truth on which the country you were born in is based upon. Learn the facts, embrace them, and move forward in truth.*

But I'm getting ahead of myself.

"I'm down, Miss Lady, Harlow," I stutter. "I am here for you and to learn from you. Know what I'm saying? I'm down for whatever you've got to give."

Harlow looks at me and takes another drag. As she inhales, she flashes me a wicked grin. "Well, then," she says. "We're gonna have one hell of a summer then, huh beautiful?"

"Hell, yeah, lady." I hold her gaze and match her grin as the road stretches out in front of us.

Chinook
Jacob Anderson-Minshall

I'm a monster. The sight of me waddling down Hawthorne Boulevard sends even the hippest of mamas pulling their children behind them, shielding their kids from me with their own bodies. Tattooed bois, dykes on bikes, pierced punkers, and homeless kids all stare at me. Their eyes dart from my belly to my face and back again. Unable to reconcile the scruffy goatee on my face with the inconceivable yet unmistakable baby bump below my flat chest, they continue to gawk.

Their eyes judge me. The sentiment spreads outward from their gaze until it encompasses their entire bodies: Lowered eyelids, knit brows, flared nostrils, Billy Idol sneers, feet shuffling backwards. They look at me the way the late Reverend Jerry Falwell would have looked at them. And they don't stop at looking. It's like they feel compelled to say *something*, like they're judges on a TV talent show and contractually obligated to criticize me. I've been called a traitor to the cause. I've been told that I've single-handedly pushed the movement back ten years. I've been told I'm *asking* for it (the it being various forms of violence). I've been told I'm going to hell and dragging others with me. I am a pregnant man.

But Tyler doesn't judge me.

Meandering through the block-sized Powell's City of Books with map in hand, I was working my way to the red room in search of *What to Expect When You're Expecting*, when I bumped into her as she left the Gay and Lesbian section.

Her sea green eyes bored right through me, stripped me down, and I stood there, naked, in front of her. And then she just walked away, leaving me exposed to the world. I was stunned. I thought we'd had a moment.

Maybe she didn't feel it. Maybe she didn't recognize me as a kindred spirit. I'd been getting that a lot. Ever since I became a man.

I couldn't get her out of my mind. Her striking eyes, her delicate bone structure and pink lips. Her features seemed all the more feminine accentuated by the veil of thick, curly hair that swaddled the lower half of her face.

She amazed me. Imagine the cultural pressure to shave! How could this woman walk around with her head held high, with utter confidence in her womanhood? Where did she get that inner strength? And how could I get some of it, extract it, condense it down to an elixir and dose myself every morning?

"Shaving would be a statement of hopelessness," I overheard her saying the next time I saw her—at Friday night Dirty Queer. I'd arrived at In Other Words a little late and, like always, the place was packed with young hip queers of every flavor. I dropped a fiver in the jar and started squeezing my way toward the bathroom when I saw her sitting on the couch. After taking care of business I hovered nearby, eavesdropping and trying to get the nerve to introduce myself. Tyler said that for her, shaving was like keeping secrets. "It requires so much energy, it's not worth it," she said. "It's debilitating. Like lying."

You've got to love a woman who thinks lying is too much trouble. It made me want to share all of my secrets with her, expose every hidden piece of myself. I barely listened to the open mic that night. Each author's voice blended into the next, then faded into white background noise. I listened to Tyler. And when she fell quiet, listening to the poets weaving colorful descriptors of queer sex, I stared at her. When her eyes met mine, I tried to silently convey my life's story to her.

I was born under the sign of water on a small farm near Eagle Creek, Oregon. By the time I started kindergarten, I knew I wasn't like the other kids. Even at that age they all seemed to share an understanding about societal norms that I wouldn't learn until well into my twenties.

By the time puberty struck, I knew what the problem was. I blamed my parents. Utilitarian to the core, my folks wouldn't tolerate any frivolity. There was simply too much work on the farm to justify wasting time on foolishness. My mother, for example, cut her own hair, never wore make-up or jewelry, and always dressed in the sensible farmer uniform—flannel shirt, jeans, and boots.

In a similar vein, my parents decided I could do without the corruptive and distractive element of television. I don't mean that they limited my viewing hours or blocked certain channels. I don't mean that we didn't have a satellite or get cable and were limited to three snowy local channels on a black and white rabbit-eared TV. I mean, there was not a television set anywhere on our property. Period.

Pop culture, my folks believed, rotted the mind and enticed kids to grow up and leave the farm. They might have been right. But being without TV didn't prevent me from fleeing as soon as I was able.

Being raised without music videos, television shows, cable movies, or rental films, was kind of like growing up in a country foreign to my neighbors and classmates. Part of what it means to *be* an American is to watch TV. Television has surpassed a public school education as the primary indoctrination tool through which children are exposed to American culture and socialized into proper American behaviors. But it's not just that. Television has become *the* medium through which children learn to recognize what is human—the breadth and diversity of the human experience. Without it, especially in rural Oregon, you get a warped, monochromatic sense of humanity and a limited understanding of natural diversity.

When I left home, I discovered it wasn't just a pop cultural education I'd missed out on, but I'd also been shielded from visual depictions of sexuality and violence. Because I had (thank god) been allowed to read—after the sun went down and all the chores were done—I'd devoured books by the handful and had squirreled away some with rather blue content. Still, their descriptions, or my imagination, didn't prepare me for actually *seeing* similar events unfold on big and small screens.

When I was finally exposed to television and movie violence, it completely shocked me. I had developed no tolerance for it. I had to cover my eyes and ears. Sometimes I had to leave, fleeing from theaters and living rooms when things turned particularly violent. I couldn't watch R rated movies. For days afterward, I couldn't shake the images from my head. I was left feeling shell shocked, as though my skin had been stripped away leaving all my nerve endings exposed.

Nor was I prepared for the noise. It seemed other people could tune it out, treat the cacophony like simple white noise and have deep meaningful conversations while the TV blared in the background. Not me.

Raised on the banks of Eagle Creek, a tributary to the mighty Columbia River, it's not surprising that the salmon were much more to me than just fish. They were like another people, a tribe that migrated up river each spring and was welcomed home like a long-lost relative. During spawning season my father would often guide fishing trips to supplement our income, and fresh caught salmon supplemented our meals.

Still, in my family, we held a certain amount of awe for the salmon and their return, the way they could fight their way upstream to the exact location of their birth. It was magical.

We never *wanted* their numbers to dwindle. And yet, we profited from their demise. The water that fed our fields was stolen from them, and when the giant pumps sucked the water from Eagle Creek other things came with it—including the aquatic insects salmon ate. Some of the fingerling salmon themselves were caught up in the suction and flung from sprinklers onto our fields, their rotting corpses adding fertilizer to our soil.

One of the culprits in the rapid decline of Columbia River salmon has been the half dozen hydroelectric dams along its course that have blocked millions of fish from accessing the higher reaches. Dams have also transformed the river into a series of slackwater reservoirs in which salmon have difficulty surviving. Other fish perish in the massive turbines used to generate some of the cheapest electricity in the world.

I often identified with the salmon, especially the Chinook that passed our farm. Maybe it's my Piscean nature, maybe it's the way my life seems to have paralleled the salmon life cycle.

As juveniles, Chinook leave their homes and travel downstream, following the Columbia River to the ocean, where they'll spend eight years roaming the seas in search of food. Traditionally, one of the salmon's richest hunting grounds has been off California's north coast where an upwelling of nutrients supports a rich ecosystem.

Salmon are andromonous; they live part of their life in fresh water and part of it in salt water. This may not seem miraculous at first, but it would be like the air around us suddenly altering from the oxygen-rich mixture we breathe to one rich in another gas like carbon dioxide; most things couldn't survive. Somehow, the salmon do. They're able to go from living in shallow sunlit birth streams to the deep dark waters of the ocean were they'll spend most of their lives.

In order to survive in such disparate environments, salmon must undergo two significant transitions. The first of which is a process called smoltification, which takes place just before the salmon enter the ocean. In river estuaries, where fresh river water mingles with the salt water from the ocean, salmon undergo the physical transformation that allows them to switch from freshwater to saltwater.

Increased levels of certain hormones cause the fish to bulk up, while deposits of crystals form on their scales turning them silver—a color that is an advantage in the ocean environment.

The changes don't stop on the physical level. Instead, those transformations lead to modification in social behavior. Their entire social organization transitions from small territorial bands to larger tribes of salmon who hail from different geographical backgrounds.

As a teenager, I too left home to find my fortune and myself. I ended up in Northern California, undergoing a complete transformation in the San Francisco Bay Area, where not only fresh and salt water, but also land and sea, and queer and straight, co-mingle. There, I became an entirely different person. My body changed so much that former friends don't recognize me. The physical changes were the most obvious to others, but they were just the tip of the iceberg.

My girlfriend at the time, a reluctant observer to my metamorphosis, described me as going 'dull.' She said all the colors had drained away, leaving me emotionally flat and drab like the gray of a dead Chinook on the deck of a seafaring fishing rig, its scales dry, no longer reflecting rainbows in their iridescent sheen. That's how I looked to her.

I experienced it differently. The first few years of undergoing gender reassignment can be like being thrown back in time and forced to go through puberty all over again. For those who enjoyed their high school years, this probably sounds like a pleasant experience. For those who disliked high school, it's torture. I *hated* high school.

Testosterone literally thickens one's skin. The epidermis loses sensitivity, pores widen, and the skin becomes rough and bumpy to the touch. No longer could I feel the touch of my lover when her soft fingertips brushed my skin like a summer's breeze. The tips of *my* fingers became thick and calloused, their sensory nerves smothered under an extra membrane of skin cells. My new skin shielded me from the world as if I were gloved, head to toe, in a layer of latex.

I was relieved. The dulling of my senses carried over to my emotions, shortening their spectrum, with the extremes simply dropping away. Everything evened out. I can still cry, but I just don't have to very often. Testosterone is like an injection of pure adrenalin. I was suddenly very active, outgoing, rushing forward, bypassing foreplay and seduction for home runs and quick release.

I was no longer damaged by imagery, not even sexually violent or degrading content, which suddenly sent jolts of electricity to my crotch. In fact, all the sensitivity I lost elsewhere seemed to have drained downward and pooled between my thighs. Gazing at women I would catch myself literally imagining them as body parts—ass, breast, mouth.

It was no surprise to me when my girlfriend left. Even after I became a man she still considered herself a good lesbian and she was getting a lot of flack from her friends about seeing a guy—even one who still had most of his lady parts. With my sexual appetite awakened I saw the breakup as freedom to sow my suddenly wild oats and play the field without a referee calling off-sides.

For the first time in my life, I actually switched teams for a season. I soon discovered that playing with boys changed the very nature of the game. I enjoyed the energy-burning playbook the boys followed, but I never really lost my love of the more cooperative game playing that happened when women entered the stadium.

It's true that I didn't give a lot of thought to the risks involved in playing such a physically demanding sport. That doesn't mean I forgot to wear protective gear—I *never* entered the ring without gloves. But I did assume that when testosterone therapy interrupted my cycle it had rendered me effectively sterile. I was wrong.

Banging boys when you've still got fallopian tubes on board is a dangerous game of chance. And apparently I don't always have the best luck. Even the thickest condom can fail.

Have you seen those little yellow caution signs, "Baby on Board?" They're meant to stick to a car window, as though the knowledge that an infant is in the vehicle will be enough to prevent another driver from say, getting behind the wheel drunk one night, running a red light and plowing into the side of the booster seat. I've always thought the idea was patently ridiculous. Until now.

While it is clearly the sight of my belly, bulging in the unmistakable globe-like curve of pregnancy, which elicits the fear and hatred I engender, that same baby bulge rescues me from suffering the ultimate punishment meted out by those patrolling the borders of appropriate behavior. My pregnancy spared me the fate of being tied spread eagle to a wooden fence and beaten to death.

I am a pregnant man, but not the famous one—you know, the trans guy who was on all the daytime talk shows and in that famous photograph, flat-chested and big bellied. He decided to get pregnant because his wife couldn't conceive. I got pregnant by accident. But don't kid yourself. Having this baby is *all* about choice. The hardest choice of all, some would say, but I couldn't imagine making a different one.

Within a month my doctor told me two things that would change my life forever. The first, about cells forming in my womb, was cause for celebration. The second, about cells forming in my breast tissue, was less so. It's funny how one tiny clump of cells is the first indication of life, while a similarly sized lump is the first sign of death. I have breast cancer and it's killing me.

People assume that female to male chest reconstruction surgery removes all of the breast tissue. It doesn't. Surgeons leave some of the material behind to mold into the pectoral shape of a man's chest. After surgery, the doctor sends some of the breast tissue to a lab to check for problem cells. They found some in my sample.

Radiation therapy was out of the question, the doctor said, if I intended to keep the baby. I had no intention of giving up my child, not even for the joys of radiation therapy. Besides, I'd already lost enough hair—an unwelcome side effect of testosterone.

"Hair is a symbol of power," Tyler says. I figure as a bearded lady, she knows. "Men are afraid of losing theirs, that's why they don't want women to have too much of it in too many places."

There's a certain power in the way she commands attention. People stare at us wherever we go. She's familiar with public performances—not because she's a circus freak, but because every time she's out in public people stop and stare and insist she explain herself. "What are you?" they ask. She's on display. Sometimes she waves, bending her hand at the wrist the way rodeo queens do when they're rounding the arena, prancing around like they're well-trained horses.

People say stupid things around us, as though something about us temporarily suspends the laws of polite society.

"At least we don't have freak shows anymore," they say.

I ask them when they last watched daytime talk shows.

"I live in a liminal place," Tyler says.

"In between what and what?" I ask, knowing myself to be a liminal kind of guy, currently lost in translation somewhere between the ill defined sexes, half woman and half man. When I join women of size in the chlorinated water of the Peninsula Pool, I become something else, half human, half fish, like a fetus, or like the transgenic frakenfish the EPA allows grocery stores to sell without even putting on a different sticker. They've spliced human genes into tomatoes, too—maybe even the ones that sparked the latest salmonella outbreak.

I read on the Internet that while you can get salmonella from eating undercooked salmon, etiologically, the first has nothing to do with the latter. Salmonella was named after a pathologist Daniel Elmer Salmon, not the leaping fish.

Tyler's laugh is like the sound of a spring gurgling out of the ground. She smiles. "Liminal also means 'in a doorway, dawn or dusk.' It's a very lovely place to be."

I stopped taking testosterone when I moved to Portland three months ago and started experiencing a bit of a reverse transition when my ovaries kicked into estrogen production overdrive. Still, a lot of things won't go back to the way it was before I became a man—like the stubble on my cheeks, the lowered voice, the thinned hair.

Pregnancy is so much a total transformation that it reminds me of transitioning. Just like when I became a man, at one point the pregnancy hormones completely took over my body and changed me from the inside out. It's incredible what the human body can do, how flexible it is, how given different hormonal and biochemical cues it can either be a man or a woman or carry another person within.

The baby inside me is liminal, too. She swims circles in my womb and when she's born she'll experience something like the salmon's smoltification.

During birth, babies produce more stress hormones than any other time in life. These hormones will enable my daughter—who Tyler let me name Chinook—to transition to life outside the womb once she's been untethered from the umbilical cord, her former life support, and handed to her new life support—the bearded lady who has promised to raise her when I'm gone.

In the meantime, her namesake salmon, the Chinook, are on their way back up the river on their spring run. After spending eight years roaming the ocean, they've come home, first stopping where the Columbia River meets the sea to undergo another round of alterations that enables them to swim upriver and spawn in freshwater. Males shift in color from demure silver to deep gaudy red, their mouths distort into the curved beaks of eagles. Despite their latest transformation, they haven't returned to their juvenile selves. You can never really go back. The fresh water, once essential to their survival, is now slowly killing them. It's a one-way journey back to their spawning grounds where, after depositing their eggs and milt, the Chinook will undergo their final transition—the one that also awaits me.

When my time is done and I'm tucked away in a silver pitcher, the dead Chinook will continue to feed an entire food chain, bringing minerals from the ocean that will sink into the soils and eventually end up in the aquatic insects that feed the next generation. I hope they'll be running up this river when my daughter undergoes her own transitions.

Where I'm From

J.T. Neel

I met Rocky my first week at the Star E. Rose Café on Alberta Street. I'd been in Portland for two rainy months and it had been exactly three weeks since I'd broken up with the boy I'd followed here. I was living in a room I found in the *Oregonian.* One of my housemates kept a padlock on her bedroom door when she was out. Most nights I found her in the kitchen, smothering toast with Nutella or peanut butter, sometimes adding a layer of sliced banana. She succumbed to brief, awkward moments of small talk before scurrying off to her room to smoke pot and watch movies with her cat.

It was my second day at the café. As I forced a cold metal scoop into a bucket of hard ice cream, I heard the jangle of the metal bell on the front door. A girl made her way behind the counter. "Did I leave my cigarettes here?"

She had spiky green hair, a septum and an eyebrow piercing, a faded denim jacket that had "FUCK IT" stenciled on the back with black and metallic gold spray paint.

"Hi," I said, a little annoyed at her sudden appearance behind the counter.

"Oh, hi," she said, feeling underneath the cash register. "I work here. I'm Rocky."

I looked down. Chocolate ice cream splattered all over the front of my shirt. I turned the mixer off, darted over to stop the steam wand from screaming into a tin pitcher of whole milk, and lopped spoonfuls of hot foam into a paper cup.

"Here they are!" A big smile spread across her face as she held the pack toward me. "Have you had a break or anything? You need a break. Come outside with me."

I handed the milkshake and the cappuccino to the mom who was waiting with her little boy. We were all looking at Rocky. She was the kind of person you looked at.

"But there's no one else to work the counter."

"It'll be fine—trust me." She grabbed my hand before I could say anything, I melted into a sweaty clam in her callused palm, and the screen door slammed behind us.

A cigarette was already dangled, unlit, out of the corner of Rocky's mouth. She jerked her hand away to fish around in her pockets, then patted herself down. She found a pink Bic lighter in a pocket of her jean jacket. I noticed a couple of greasy, long-haired guys sitting in green plastic chairs outside, each straddling a hand drum. They had been there the day before. "What's your name?" she asked, her eyebrows were furrowed and one hand cupped the end of her cigarette. The wind shuffled through my short, messy hair, while her crisp green spikes stood straight up.

"Samantha," I said.

"You just moved here?"

"Yeah, how'd you know?"

She smiled into the distance, squinted at the sun, blew the smoke into the sky. "You're dating that poet boy, aren't you?"

Anonymity had been the only benefit of my loneliness. I felt it sucked from under me as Rocky took another drag. I remembered the poem my ex had read at the café's open mic last month.

"We weren't really dating," I said. "Anyway, we broke up."

"Are you a dyke?"

My shoe was untied. I fought the urge to tie it. I looked at Rocky, and opened my mouth. Nothing came out. Where I'm from, the word dyke is an insult, a precursor to violence. "No. I don't know," I declared uncertainly.

"Where are you from?" she asked.

"The Ozarks."

"Where's *that*?" she raised an eyebrow.

"Well, I'm from Arkansas, but the Ozark Mountains are also in southern Missouri. And they're a little bit in Oklahoma and Kansas, too. Have you ever read *Where the Red Fern Grows*? The book about the little boy and his two dogs? That story took place in the Ozarks."

She took another drag, studied my face with squinted eyes. "Interesting," was all she said.

She looked down the sidewalk, waved at someone walking a pit bull. The dog had a studded collar and a red handkerchief around its neck. The dog's owner waved back and smiled. I couldn't tell if they were a boy or a girl.

"Where are *you* from?" I asked.

"California." She smashed her cigarette with her pink Converse sneaker and tossed it the trash can. "I gotta go," she said. "Band practice. See ya later." She took off in the direction of the boy/girl and the dog.

I bent down to tie my shoe.

As I reached for the screen door to head back into the cafe, she yelled back at me: "You know about the party tonight, right? I'll stop by at the end of your shift and we'll go together!"

It was a dance party in Northeast, on Prescott, and she seemed to know everyone. She weaved in and out of groups, saying hello, giving high-fives. She wrestled a friend to the ground on the grass. I trailed behind her and every once in a while she said, "Oh, yeah. This is Samantha." Her friends gave me suspicious looks or quick nods before moving on to socialize with people they knew. Pretty soon Rocky was making out with someone up against the side of the house, and I was alone. I'd never seen two girls making out before.

I stood by the fire-pit and watched the tall flames that leapt from it, flickering light on faces I'd never seen. Next to me was a handsome girl with short black hair and long eyelashes. On the other side of the fire was a girl in striped leggings and a denim miniskirt and silver hoop earrings that danced like fireflies against her neck. I sat on a stump and warmed my hands and feet. I didn't want to go back to that room I'd found in the *Oregonian*.

I was born in a small town, graduated high school with the same kids I went to kindergarten with. The public school had been built in the early part of the century, was made of stone and mortar, religion and ghosts. We weren't allowed to wear shorts, even when temperatures reached over one hundred degrees. The principal banned school dances because he and his church considered dancing a sin, said it was the devil's work. Boys were allowed to skip school during hunting season, as long as they came back with a good story.

We pledged allegiance every morning as the flag was unfolded and raised. We sang about Jesus. It was expected that I would live, work, get married, and die in that town—or at least in a nearby county.

Almost everyone stuck around after high school. "And those ones that leave, well, they might as well stay gone 'cause they never gonna come back the same," my uncle said at Thanksgiving, while he watched a fuzzy football game on TV and spat chewing tobacco into a Styrofoam cup.

After high school, my best friend dropped her plans for college, moved in with her high school sweetheart, and got a secretarial job in town.

Angela and Tony's courtship had persisted through our junior and senior years. They spent weekends running around town in his pickup truck, smoking Marlboro Reds and making promises. They parked his truck under the thick foliage of a weeping willow, just around the bend from her parent's farm, and had sex. At school on Monday, Angela gave me the updates. She'd slam her biology book down on the table, toss back her permed sandy brown hair, and say, "We started having butt sex. It hurts, but it's alright." She was the only girl who talked to me about sex and I was all ears. For others, there was something unspeakable about my lack of experience.

The fall of our junior year, when I still didn't have a boyfriend, Angela sometimes invited me to drive around town with her and Tony in his pickup truck. Tony was a senior with a reputation. He punched kids at lunchtime and everyone knew he had pot in his locker. He saved his money from summer construction jobs and bought Angela gold earrings on her birthday, roses on Valentine's Day, a black leather jacket for Christmas. Angela was a good church-going farm girl by day, but after her parents went to sleep, she took the four-wheeler out and went to Tony's. Once, her purse spilled out on the newly waxed kitchen floor, a pink compact of birth control pills and a half-smoked pack of Marlboros slid across the linoleum. Her mom pretended not to see.

One Friday night, when Tony came to pick us up, we had to wait while Angela faced off with her dying perm, armed with a comb, curling iron, and a bottle of Aqua Net in the bathroom. I sat in the porch swing and Tony smoked cigarettes and paced. The wooden planks creaked under the weight of his boots.

When we got in the truck, he eased down the gravel driveway, onto the dirt road, and just as we were out of eyesight of her parents' house, his foot got heavy and he gunned it down the road. The truck skidded around turns, barreled down the dirt road, and left behind a tunnel of burnt orange dust. When we reached the fork in the road, he peeled out onto the highway going north and Angela lit a cigarette. I sat there, watching the pastures stretch out in brown and green quilt squares, towards the dark rolling hills. In fifteen minutes, we'd be in town and I could get out of the truck.

"God-dammit Angela, I told you to put that CD back in its case. Now it's scratched!" When the stoplight turned green, his snake skin boots stepped on the gas so hard our heads launched back into the headrests.

"I'll get you a new one, honey," Angela said softly.

I held my breath and glared out the window, waiting for his mood to be done. I looked at the neon signs we sped past. Dairy Queen. The Dollar Spot. The Holiday Inn.

Angela, who was hard-headed and never let anyone tell her what to do, got soft when Tony was angry. "He has a hard home life," she explained. "His step-dad treats him like shit."

We found Tony's friends in a parking lot in front of the Christian bookstore. Tony parked and we sat on the tailgate. Some of them were seniors and some were drop outs. They wore pointed cowboy boots and dirty jeans with circles of denim faded into white on the back pockets, where they kept their cans of Skoal. They blasted Black Sabbath and Metallica, cussed and laughed and talked shit about rich kids, started fights and glared at the cops who drove by. Some of them had girlfriends with long bleached hair and eyes outlined with thick crusts of black eyeliner. Their girlfriends glared at girls they didn't know, snuck out of their houses at night and smoked cigarettes at church camp. Those girls didn't acknowledge me.

I sat stiffly on the tailgate, sipped on a bottle of Jack Daniels when it was passed to me, not sure where I fit in.

That night, when he was driving us back to Angela's house, Tony was the one who broke the spell of silence. "You're too quiet. Gives me the creeps. Why don't you say something every once in a while?"

I looked at Angela, and she shrugged, took a drag off his cigarette, flicked it in the ashtray, and handed it back to him. I took a sip of whiskey and watched the dogwoods whiz past.

"So, ya never had a boyfriend, have ya?" I felt a flame rise to my cheeks, dousing my neck with heat.

"No," I admitted quietly. I remembered back to being a little kid, when I told my mom I was a boy, and the shame I felt when she corrected me.

"What you need… is a good 'ol boy."

I laughed nervously.

"What do you think about Sean? He's kinda cute, huh? He doesn't talk much, either."

I thought he was cute, but I couldn't imagine him and me. I took another sip of whiskey and hoped that Sean would try to kiss me someday soon, and prove me and everyone else wrong.

"Leave her alone, Tony. She doesn't like Sean."

I didn't say anything, just bit my lip and stepped on an imaginary brake as we rounded the bend near Angela's house.

"I guess I'm taking you two home," Tony said bitterly as we passed the willow tree.

As Angela and Tony kissed goodbye in the truck, I waited in the front yard, next to the barn. I felt a little drunk, and laid down on the grass.

I heard Tony's truck easing back down the gravel driveway and the sliding glass door open, and Angela said in an aggravated whisper, "What's wrong? Are you coming in or not?"

The door slid shut as I started to say, "Nothing's wrong." But the words got caught in my throat, cramped by the tight loneliness of a lie.

After my first relationship in Portland ended, I considered going back to Arkansas, but I couldn't imagine myself there.

Rocky had warned me: "Your first breakup with a girl is always the hardest."

But her words gave me little comfort. Like Rocky herself, who took me under her wing for my first four months in Portland, only to leave without warning—San Francisco, then Philly, then New York.

"I never stay in one place too long," she said. "Didn't I tell you that?"

It was hard to lose my only friend in this rainy city.

I called her in San Francisco. I could hear Bikini Kill blasting in the background.

"Hey Samantha, how are you?"

"I think I might go back," I announced.

I could hear people talking and laughing. She yelled to someone, "Hey, the CD's skipping."

"Samantha, if you're gonna go back there, I'm not coming to your funeral, OK?"

"What do you mean?"

"You know what I mean," she said.

I knew.

Her friend had put on a Johnny Cash CD now. It reminded me of home. My dad and I used to listen to Johnny Cash when I was a kid.

Soon I forgot about going back. I moved out of my house, into a house with some queers I met at a party. New friends gravitated to me. It was spring, and still raining, but there were tulips everywhere and the fruit trees bloomed along the sidewalk. Cherry blossoms littered the streets like pink confetti and stuck to my bike tires. There were patches of blue between billowy white clouds. The reappearance of the sun gave me amnesia about winter. And because it was so difficult to reconcile the two worlds, I tried to forget about where I came from.

After four years in Portland, I was tired of hiding parts of my life from my family, so I sent a coming-out email.

When I called a few days later, I could tell by the way my mom answered the phone that she hadn't come to terms with the email.

I was curled up in a musty green armchair. My room was makeshift, with only a curtain dividing it from the kitchen.

"Of course I still love you," my mom said angrily. "I just want you to be happy."

I didn't know what to say. There was no love in her voice.

"Is that why you moved to Portland?"

"To be gay?" I asked. I had to think about it. "No."

"Do you think you were born this way, or is this a lifestyle you've chosen?"

"I don't know how to answer that," I said.

"Well, is this a phase, or do you think you could get married to a man and have children someday?"

Her questions stopped needing answers, were merely stray bullets of her disappointment.

"Aren't you afraid you're going to get AIDS?" my mother finally asked, her voice shaking.

I hung up, buried my face in the armchair.

I could have told someone about the phone call, but I didn't. I didn't want to explain to anyone that I had sympathy for my mom. That I knew where she was coming from. I didn't think anyone would understand.

Two years deep into a relationship and several pronouns later, I asked my parents to visit me in Portland.

"Your daddy can't come." My mom sighed as she handed the phone to him.

"Someone's gotta feed the dogs and take care of things around here," he said. The truth was that my dad had never set foot on an airplane, and never would. We all knew it, but we let him tell his own story.

It was the first time my mom had seen me with a girl. I really wanted her to like Syd, and I wanted her to see that I was happy. I wanted to use the words "queer" and "genderqueer" in casual conversation, to help her get past the flinching stage when she heard those words.

She wanted to tour rose gardens and go to Powell's.

Syd drove us to Astoria. My mom took scores of pictures of the sea lions with her new digital camera and stood on the beach and smiled at the ocean. She didn't take any pictures of me and Syd. When we made eye contact, she was always the first to look away. Our language was logistical, consisted of directions and menu choices. And I kept my pronouns to myself.

Later in the week, I took her to Alberta Park so we could talk. We sat on a bench near the playground. I told her I wanted to talk about how she was dealing with me being gay. "It's pretty big, Mom. You came out here for the first time. You just met my partner of two years. You must have some feelings about it."

She sat stiffly, hands on her thighs. Her feet didn't quite reach, but dangled a couple of inches off the ground. She swung them back and forth a few times, then stopped. "Well, I just want you to be happy," she said sharply.

"Well, I am happy. But I think you might have some other emotions, too. I know it's a hard process. You seem to be having a good time, but you won't even look at me."

She turned to me, her eyes brimming with tears. "You're the one who left! We didn't desert you. You decided to move way out here and become this person I don't even know anymore."

I'd rarely seen my mom lose her composure before. So many feelings had been bottle-necked behind her polite smile.

"I'm the same person, Mom," I said. "I'm more myself than ever, if you want to know the truth."

"You just can't expect me to understand. No parent would ever want their child to be gay. That's just a fact."

"That. Is not. True." I clenched my jaw.

"Yes it is. No parent could want that for their child. It's not possible."

"Yes it is! I have friends whose parents embrace the fact that they're gay. I have friends whose parents *are* gay! Just because you're having a hard time with it doesn't mean that's how everyone else feels."

"Of course not. I told you I accept you for who you are."

"You mean you tolerate me."

"You're being impossible, Samantha."

"My name is Sam." I hadn't corrected her all weekend. It felt good to say it.

"Samantha, I gave you your name. Why are you ashamed of who you were?" She put her hands over her face to hide the tears. Then she looked up at me, cheeks wet with tears. "Do you want to be a man or something?"

I became incredibly aware of the tightness of my binder. She shifted her gaze upward, and began to reassemble herself again. Two fingers wiped just underneath each eye with forceful, even strokes. She examined her fingers, and wiped the wet mascara tears on her jeans. I had never seen my mom's makeup out of place before.

She wasn't ready to hear the complicated truth about my gender. "No, mom," I said.

After a few moments of silence, she spoke again. "You don't understand where I live," she said. "There's no one for me to talk to. Homosexuals just aren't accepted there." She took a deep breath. " I see it's fine for you here." She waved her hand around at the park. "You can get away with it in this city, probably in other cities, too. But it's just not tolerated where I'm from."

"I know, Mom. I'm from that place, too."

The morning of my mom's departure, I felt sad and relieved, a thick knot swelling in my throat. As I drove home from PDX, I realized something that had escaped me all week.

It was one of those moments when every group of cells in your body startles at once—a sudden collective realization of what a few cells knew all along.

It was possible that my mom would always wince at hearing the word "queer." I couldn't soften the sharp edges of the word for her. I couldn't edit the content of it for her. I couldn't always keep the pronouns safely hidden.

"Queer," I said aloud, like an affirmation at the stoplight on Killingsworth and 42nd. I liked the sound of it, the way it rolled off my tongue.

As I turned left on 33rd, I rolled the window down. I passed New Seasons, the friendliest store in town. Voted the best place to cruise dykes in Northeast in a recent poll.

"Queer!" I yelled out the window.

There was a guy putting a sack of groceries in his car, a woman crossing the parking lot with a shopping cart. They both glanced over at me, but neither flinched.

Will the Circle Be Unbroken

Donal Mosher

16th St., San Francisco

The clinic door closes. Yes, it's cancer. It's probably treatable if I can get money or find a free experimental treatment. Yes, fog can turn to ash—I can see it happening on the hills above the Castro district. A body can pass through a solid substance—each step I take along the sidewalk, I'm waiting for it to happen.

Mirabel Ave., Bernal Hill, San Francisco

Old songs, old voices, reconciling death with images of the dark river Jordan, the angel band gathering, the streets of gold. It's not the promise of heaven these songs offer, but a desire for something eternal, right here and now. If the treatments don't work, if coping with the disease becomes the measure of my life, then I want the touch of angels. I want their voices. I want to walk the gleaming streets that sprawl out beyond the high view from our kitchen.

Harrison St., New Year's Eve, San Francisco

Lost in "Can't Get You Out of My Head," a heavy, aging drag queen swings a forearm, thick and round like a freckled melon, above her head. She's been still and sharp-eyed all night, standing at the dark edge of the dance floor. Only this song puts her sequin-covered bulk in motion. Her arm catches the neck of a tiny, balding man, sweeping him into her dazzle and gravity. Her wig flies from her head as they topple. Caught in flashing light, it seems to hang for a second above them, a hairdo without a head. On the floor, she locks him in a kiss. His legs pump in ecstasy or asphyxiation. When the music changes they do not touch or speak. She resumes her place in the shadows, waiting for the next perfect song.

Market St., San Francisco

On the way home after dancing, Valium putting the "pill" in pillow, a bicycle with squeaky wheels passes. The rider raises himself off the seat to look at me, arms dangling from his black T-shirt, thin and white, the limbs of a stick figure drawn in chalk. He waits for me. "How you doing?"

"Fine," I say, but quickly add, "tired."

The conversation continues, one innuendo after another. I shoot them all down. Finally he says, honest and nice, "Look, I think you're hot. I'd like to see you naked. I'd like to smell your farts."

I blush, not at his words, but at his sincerity. When I tell him I really can't oblige, he says, "just let me see it. I'll give you twenty bucks." Half a block later I find myself behind a Zuni's dumpster, revealing my bashful goods. I feel like I owe it to him to be hard, but I'm glad I'm not. I take the twenty, politely refuse his phone number. Going up my front steps, I feel the bill curled against my thigh. It only occurs to me then that he was in pretty ragged condition and that I'd just given a twenty-buck peep show to someone who probably couldn't afford it.

Parnassus Ave., San Francisco
I call him Dr. Rubbergloves because his touch is clinging, but his voice is remote and powdery. He asks the survey questions that will grant me free treatment. Then I'm flat on my back as he secures a plastic cast of my lower body. A hollow version of me, molded from my own form. It fits perfect and does not allow me to move during treatment. "You won't feel anything," the doctor says. Machines move over me. Clicking. No I don't feel anything, but wish I did. I wish I could feel anything other than panic.

4th St., San Francisco
Lance greets me at the elevator and up we go to his apartment. Clothes off as soon as the door closes. My scrappy jeans crumbled atop his carefully folded Abercrombie & Fitch wear. He is so tall that my eye comes right up to his nipple. I could suckle him with my pupil. I'll swear it takes five minutes to look at all of him, his long swimmer's body, extended limbs, his eyes so large against his thin, fine features. His speech is clear and precise. His mind is made for math, grammar, and tax returns. When he holds me I feel I'm leaning against a great wall of waspish-ness. He's appalled and aroused by my stories of trailer life, food stamps, and chicken farming. It's a cheap thrill, this poor kid's power to titillate middle class sensibility. And when we lay down on those crisp Egyptian cotton sheets of his, it's like fucking a jungle gym.

Mirabel Ave., Bernal Hill, San Francisco
From the glass doors in the kitchen I can see the whole network of San Francisco, glittering and curving over the hills. Tiny headlights move along the dark channels of streets and avenues. My reflection is transparent in the glass. I take off my clothes and let the lights move through my limbs, my torso. Find the

cancer I ask them, burn it out gently. Eat it out Pacman style. For a second I'll swear the moving lights tickle me. Then the door downstairs clicks open, drunken housemates spilling in. They see me flashing past, shrieking and clutching a dig rag between my legs. I slam my door and fall on the bed laughing. Their laughter outside the door. My laughter. I love my body more than I have since the diagnosis.

Shotwell St., San Francisco

I'm on my way home from radiation treatment. I've gotten used to being nauseated and dizzy, but there is wrongness in my body that is not a physical symptom and has no physical location. It's the thought of the cancer, growing in the weird garden of my interior. It's the thought of radiation passing through my flesh and burning away at elements so microscopic and subtle they are akin to spirit. It is a bright, windy morning. Light falls so heavily over the street that it seems to penetrate the surface of buildings, saturating them to overflow. Static bursts from a battered radio as I pass by the basketball court. The hiss unfolds into strings and a voice crooning fervently, "Oh my love, my darling, I hunger for your touch…" Growing louder, the song takes everything on the street into itself—the game on the court; the drunks on the curb; the baby blue church flyers under my feet, each one printed with "Are you saved?" in English and Spanish. The melody flows over houses, trees, and asphalt for almost two blocks before fading and releasing the world with the words "God speed your love to me."

Albina St., Portland

The rose garden at night, raining slightly. Under the streetlight, the red and white blossoms have the rusty tint of old Kodachrome. I'm here to celebrate coming through radiation treatments. For now and maybe forever, as bodies go, the cancer is dead. I can bury it here. I make my way to the fountain at the center of the park. Wet sound rushes my ears. The garden around me is chambered like a heart. The rose stems seem to pulse—thick, thorny veins. I don't know it yet, but in two years I'll have a house three blocks away.

Harrison St., San Francisco

We met at the foot of a stage. Thick male feet squeezed into stilettos stomped and kicked over our conversation. A lip synch act I can't remember. Two years later we're riding out of San Francisco with our household jumbled up in a truck and our new home waiting in Portland. Mike is quiet. I'm waiting for the sense of departure to hit, but all I get are memories— streets, homes, beds, bodies, faces—passing through my mind, bright and rhythmic as the houses that flicker past the window. I barely notice when we leave the city behind. I'm not leaving, I'm returning.

Williams Ave., Portland

A simple church sign sliding past the car window as we drive lost around town. "WHEN LOOKING FOR FAULTS, USE A MIRROR NOT A TELESCOPE."

Kerby Ave., Portland

Boxes in every room. All of them threatening to break my heart. The Carter Family fills the house. Will the circle be unbroken? Good question. Outside I hear train whistles, a sound I haven't heard in my own home since I was a kid. It blends with the voices of Sarah and Maybelle, giving a strange depth to their flat singing, opening the distance between the speakers on the floor and the distant train yard. I see a black iron train on golden tracks, a train with engines at either end, moving both directions at once, always arriving, always leaving. The song changes. The train passes. If the better home is waiting it's in all these boxes we have to empty.

MLK, Portland

Blossoms and bit of trash blowing on the wet night wind. A marquee glows in front of a church that may have once been a fast food restaurant. Black letters against bright white, "THE DEVIL'S GREATEST WILE IS WAIT A WHILE!"

Stark St., Portland

A man in wheelchair, his legs tangled in a knot in his lap, sitting and flirting with old men and pretty boys by the window at Scandals. Outside a man in tattered, clown-like clothes stumbles and vomits on a Prius. Everyone cheers.

3rd St., Portland

At the Silverado, a man buys me a drink and tells me he doesn't come here often. He likes female strippers. He painted his house after his favorite. "Beige siding like her skin. Black trim like her hair and eye lashes. The entrance, deep burgundy." Behind him a woman about three and a half feet tall is lifted up to the stage. Her small, pearly blue, manicured nails gleam as she slips a dollar into the male stripper's briefs—black spandex with metallic spots, also gleaming. No one's watching. Spectators cast glances across the club. Eyes catch a change of light. Faces change color. An expression of tawdry confidence gains strength as it's met and reflected.

12th St., Portland

In a stranger's apartment, I tell him this is the first time I've been with anyone since meeting my boyfriend. He's nervous too but doesn't say why. We go about seduction like horny, clumsy virgins—trading innuendoes, finding excuses to show off our bodies, exchanging calculated, accidental touches. He strips down to his underwear, saying how warm the radiator is. I can see his erection beneath wash-worn cotton but he says suddenly, with a shaky voice, that he's HIV positive and not ready for sex. He tells me "I got it from my boyfriend. We used to shoot speed. He infected me with a needle because he thought it would bond us. I didn't know anything about it."

Now he's more of a stranger than when we first spoke at the bar. Did that really happen to him? Is this just a rewrite of his speed freak past? I don't know him well enough to ask these questions or believe his answers. The only clear thing is the need in his voice, though for what I don't know. Later in his bed, my balls are raging but my hands happily clasp my own shoulders. Streetlight falls over his trim body, shaking with some dream. I drift, dozing and waking, all the while noting the differences between him and the lover I know so well and share a home with. Somewhere across the river our bedroom is dark and the trains are whistling.

Kerby Ave., Portland

Mike is away and I'm alone in the house. Rain batters the windows. The whole place creaks like a ship. Lying in bed, listening to the downpour, I remember nights in San Francisco spent listening to my body. Listening for something I couldn't see or feel moving in there. I heard my skin brushing the sheet. I heard my breath, even the dim blood pulse in my ears. But I was listening for the soft footsteps of the cancer, the ghost walking inside me. Christmas lights burn outside the windows, clusters of magical hard candies, filled with light and childhood. But their bright cheer soothes me 'til I drift off and dream it's raining tiny light bulbs. They break with soft pops and spill light all over the street and yard.

Albina Ave., Portland / Mission District, San Francisco
Colored lights and dark houses bring back the memory of Christmas Eve in San Francisco when Matt called to tell me a friend of his had committed suicide. Before his death the man made a circle of Christmas lights on his kitchen floor. He'd then taken his collection of vintage stuffed animals and campy dolls and set them around the circle where I imagine they sat glowing as if in some faery ring or some enchanted tea party. He then fixed a rope to the exposed heavy pipes that ran along the ceiling and hanged himself within in his magic circle.

I couldn't stay home after that so I walked down to the Mission district. The Victorian houses above Dolores Park were vibrantly trimmed—every antique, wedding-cake detail sparkled with icicle lights. Christmas trees stood in bay windows, boughs draped with red ribbon and tiny bulbs. I thought of Dickens, of Scrooge standing unseen and unheard at the fine party, of the spirit of Marley revealing that the air of London on Christmas Eve was thicker with lost souls than with snow or soot. Down on Mission St. cheap statues of Jesus, Mary, and all the saints waited patiently in closed shop windows. In some basement club, lit only by ropes of blue lights, a woman sang old hymns in a high, sweet voice. During Wayfaring Stranger, I closed my eyes and saw a vision of the river Jordan—one bank of blood and muscle—one bank of bright gold—dark water between. As the words came, "Beauteous fields lie just before me..." I pictured thousands of fragile lights on a dark landscape—streetlights—Christmas lights—candles—"...Where God's redeemed their vigil's keep."

Kerby Ave., Portland
Gardening in the backyard, I hear Mike playing "Angel Band" inside the house. The songs carries everything I love about our

home out to me—the light falling on the wooden floor, the warm solid rooms filling with the sound of my banjo and his guitar, morning fucking, nights with his back against my chest rising as he sleeps. I haven't told him today is the three-year anniversary of my cancer diagnosis. I'm not going to. Through the trees, the low sun is a bright orb. "That's my death," I think, contented. "Right there. I could reach out and take hold of it. It could sit warm in my hand until I draw it into my heart." The soil in the vegetable bed turns under the hoe, black and flecked with star-like constellations of white gypsum.

Lombard St., Portland

A one-armed man in camouflage pants and an American flag T-shirt rides a lawn mover round a sign planted in a local church lawn. One side of the sign reads GOD IS LOVE. The other side reads LOVE IS GOD. Round he goes, moving in an ever-expanding circle.

Unlocking the Hips
David Oates

Mike

The track coach told me to watch Mike's hips, so I ran workouts right behind him. They rocked, they unlocked, those hips gave him a fluid stride and a springy strength. And lord, that sexy, flexy lower back.

Coach saw me as underperforming most of the time. It was a high school, he wanted victories, but I was trying the half-mile that year instead of my natural longer events. It was my rebellion. I wanted to be fast and powerful. The long-distance claque plods past, too skinny for words, that open-jawed hangdog look.

Mike and I are about to do repeat quarters at sixty seconds. Twelve of them. He's a year older, cool and confident. Coach whistles us on and clicks his stopwatch. Mike has a beautiful stride, efficient, self-contained, powerful. His arms ride low. Hands not clenched. At each stride, the unlocked hip rotates forward and lengthens his reach. He's running from his lower abdomen, each rotation is an uncoiling of the torso's core strength. Guys who run on legs only are left behind.

I'm a good student and I start running better almost immediately. Mike is much shorter than me, wide-shouldered, lean. His last name is Mexican. The seniors rib each other, bantering and rowdy. Laughing, they call him "nigger" in the shower room because his penis is dark. The rest of him is a light mahogany. It doesn't matter. Mike wins all his races. He's unflappable, suave. They can't touch him.

We only get a minute or two between quarter-miles. I'm deep-trained for distance and hard to tire. I stick without a word, watching Mike's hips.

Bob

"Oates, I *missed* you." His face was exasperated, and the word *missed* landed with flawless deadpan. Underneath was sincere. We had been working together for three weeks without a break, repairing the abandoned camp, sleeping in the crumby bunkhouse, eating the makeshift food. Then a week off. Now we were back—and this surprising greeting. *Who knew a straight boy could have feelings?*

I was touched but it threw off all my calculations.

Bob was not suave. Homely and skinny, he used to be a nationally ranked marathoner but neither of us was competing anymore. Now we were mountaineers. Sort of.

Once, he came and sat on the edge of my cot, an hour or two after lights out, asking if I was OK. He didn't exactly know I had finally cracked that night—tears on the pillow, frustration I almost couldn't bear. None of my calculations made me strong enough. Bob saw something. I kept meeting men who extended kindness to me, like they were unafraid. I didn't expect it, didn't know it was out there. How then should I be?

It was exasperating. The next day as we hiked along, dusty and silent, I just started laughing. I never told him why.

Carny

Santa Barbara was a hot long hitchhike from San Francisco once our spring break getaway was over. When the battered Nova stopped, I jumped in the passenger side while Harry and the backpacks took the rear. The driver—I remember thinking, *he's got a nice head of hair for such an old guy.* He said he was a carny. "You know what that is? Carny?" He shouted at us, all the windows down in the heat and doing a very noisy, bouncing-and-gliding seventy. This was on the 101, with all its patches and old paving. He gave me a huge blunt handshake and I realized he wasn't old but just *worked,* hard-worked and weathered.

He was a carnival foreman, had done it for a long time. "I've seen everything. Everything. You know?" I didn't, but guessed that I did. I never felt less menace from anyone in my life. He was almost fatherly. Or motherly. Still, I was on guard, being who I was. He talked on about the kind of men who work a carnival then drift off, the way he woke up one day and felt he had seen enough unkindness for three lifetimes.

Then he brought up Nixon. He leaned over, still not menacing but I hated to think where this would end up. We were long-haired and scared of what we called rednecks. "Stay out of that damn war. Stay in school, that's good." He asked if I knew how many Vietnamese we had killed, how many GIs. "We're going to kill a lot more before that s.o.b. is done." He wasn't arguing, just shouting over the freeway. "That Mao—in China? I know we're supposed to hate him. But you know what I think? I think he fed his people." He looked at me to see if I registered. "It's a poor country. He fed his people."

There were no stickers on his back bumper, nothing to give him away. It was late cool dusk, we were outside Atascadero, and we knew a girl to call there. The carny blinked on his lights and waved backwards at us as he pulled out.

The T'ai Chi Instructor

The t'ai chi instructor does not hurry. He is not lunging, and he's not *not* lunging.

The t'ai chi instructor is not seen as the observer wills.

The t'ai chi instructor is on the balls of his feet, shifting weight. When he pushes the air, I believe it. When he rotates, everything rotates.

The t'ai chi instructor's tummy peeks out, fuzzy, fleshy. He is not a Greek god. His T-shirt comes a little short, it's what he wore to teach a roomful of Portland strangers.

His body is not a vehicle, not an advertisement, it doesn't project anything—power, or glamour, or masculinity, or even sexiness—which of course could be quite sexy. He might be thirty, and I'm almost double that. It's my first t'ai chi ever.

It could be dancing, really. His spine is loose and his hips fluid. Not like those professional dancers on TV, those gimbled manlings, those palomino women. I don't know what that is. This is nice. Amazing.

The t'ai chi instructor is the kind of guy you can't tell what kind of guy he is. He smoothes through one move and connects it to the next. I'm so bad at this it should bother me. But think how good I must make the others feel. I've had good teachers, and he's another. He bends, uncoils, there's that lower-abdomen place again. All the power is in there, behind the fuzz. For a while, I ran from that place.

I'm the stiffest person in the room, but I feel a willow. Bull-willow. Sissy-willow. I might get better at this, who knows?

Masturbate Theater
Marc Acito

Question: Where do you find hot men in Portland?
Answer: San Francisco.

Visitors from gay meccas are often shocked by the low-key (some say low-grade) quality of the local lads. Due to the weather, we can be a pale, doughy bunch. What's more, Portland's queers have long been well integrated in the greater community, which means it can be hard to tell the gay guys from the straight ones. Or the lesbians. Depending on how you feel about the Adonis worship inherent in gay culture, our men can seem refreshingly real or depressingly drab. Personally, while I'm relieved not to feel like the runt of the litter when I'm in a bar, there's something distressing about being in better shape than the go-go boys.

So I welcome the chance to migrate south in the winter, letting it all hang out at one of the clothing-optional resorts in Palm Springs. Y'know, the kind of place where you can lie around naked and talk about the first thing that pops up.

I'm poolside at the aptly named INNdulge when I notice an item in the aptly named *Bottom Line*: "Pornstar BBQ & Video Shoot, Saturday 1:00 p.m., All Worlds Resort."

"What do you suppose they serve at a porn star barbecue?" I ask my partner.

"Foot long hot dogs, I guess," he says.

I'm kind of conflicted about porn. On the one hand, I think it can be dehumanizing, an obstacle to intimacy. On the other hand...well, porn can keep the other hand pretty busy.

So I figure, what the hell? I'm on vacation. And, as a writer, I take a subversive pleasure in knowing I can legitimately use the admission fee as a tax deduction.

They're actually barbecuing hamburgers when I arrive, but the porn stars are the ones handling the meat, which only seems appropriate. Aaron Tanner, a former financial advisor and today's bottom, works the grill. I'm introduced to him by his real name, which only serves to confuse me. I have a hard enough time remembering names as it is.

I ask Aaron how much he makes a shoot, so to speak.

"That's a personal question," he sniffs.

I see. Taking pictures usually reserved for the proctologist is OK, but asking about finances—that's too invasive.

A production assistant stands up on a chair to address the crowd of about sixty men gathered on the patio. "Today we'll be filming *Pornstruck 4*," he says. For those of you who may have missed *Pornstrucks 1-3*, they're all about naked men having sex at a resort in Palm Springs.

Pornstruck 4 is a decidedly low budget affair—one camera, one light, a lot of condoms and a Costco-sized bottle of lube with a pump top. There's no fluffer, despite numerous volunteers from the audience. Aaron does the honors for his co-star, whose porn name is Tino Lopez, not to be confused with Tina Louise, TV's "Ginger" from *Gilligan's Island*.

I kneel down to get a better view of the action and notice at least a half dozen guys in the crowd playing pocket pool. But the sex doesn't do a thing for me. Granted, I'm not going anywhere until it's over, but I'm not aroused. It's just not as sexy without the editing and the wompa wompa music.

Rafael, the director (one name only please, like Madonna or Cher), films the blow jobs first, which take an hour or so, then sets up the rim shots. "OK, spread 'em," he instructs Tino. The entire crowd moves forward *en masse* in anticipation. "Now DIVE!" he shouts like a submarine commander. Perhaps they should call this movie *Das Booty* instead. I glance sideways and note that lots of periscopes are up.

"OK," the PA announces, "we'll be back in fifteen minutes for penetration." A statement you don't hear every day.

The penetration shots take a long time and the crowd grows restless. In between takes Aaron swigs Mountain Dew and rubs Anbusol on his ass to numb the irritation. (You try getting screwed for hours on end without chafing). Tino changes to a fresh condom every time we break. I don't know why, he just likes it that way.

Aaron does his cum shot, then fakes an orgasm three more times for the close-ups, like Meg Ryan in *When Harry Met Sally*. "Don't wipe that up," Rafael says to the PA, "we need that for the next shot." (Continuity is so important in filmmaking).

But Tino is having trouble delivering the goods and Aaron has to lie there all sticky while he waits for Tino to finish. A cell phone goes off. Guys in the crowd start looking at their watches and muttering about dinner reservations. I'm reminded of the time I went to Cape Canaveral and had to wait a really long time before the rocket finally launched.

Tino is sent to the bathroom to concentrate.

"Clear a space," the PA says, "when he's ready, he'll come running." Or perhaps cum running. But alas, it seems the old well's done run dry. Tino can't finish.

"We'll do the cum shot tomorrow," the PA announces to

the few of us remaining. Most of the guys in audience have wandered off, some going back to their rooms to do what poor Tino cannot. The rest of us gather around a cute blond with a bulge at his crotch so engorged he looks like he shoplifted an eggplant.

At the urging of someone in the crowd (OK, it was me), he reveals the goods, to the appreciative murmurs from the crowd.

"You should do the movie," I say.

"Nah, I'm too shy," he says, stuffing himself back into his pants. "I only act like this when I'm out of town."

"Really? Where are you from?"

He smiles, embarrassed. "Portland."

FOR SERVICE AND DEVOTION

Lesbian Landscaping
Sarah Dougher

When I moved from Portland to Olympia in January, the only job I could find was with the company everyone called "lesbian landscapers." This was not their real name. My first day was Valentine's Day. That morning when we woke up, my girlfriend told me that moving to Olympia, that moving into her house, had been a bad idea. It made her feel trapped and like she never wanted to have sex again. She lived on an acre, all lawn. She tended it with a riding mower. The mower had been a gift from her last girlfriend, an extravagant if practical last attempt at love.

On my first day, I woke up and made tea. My girlfriend stayed in bed, it was still early. I was getting picked up in the crew truck at seven and it was barely light. I took my tea in a plastic cup when Lisha arrived and honked the horn. Lisha was my boss, ten years my junior.

Lisha grew up south of Olympia on Chase Road. Her mom married twice, and a third time when she was nine to the man she calls her dad. Her mom was named Jane. "She's a firey redhead." These were the first things Lisha told me when I got in the truck.

Portland's vague opportunities and complexities receded quickly when I made the choice to move to Olympia: So sweet and small, full of gardeners and artists. Upon arriving, I realized I was frightened of the spaces there, the deep forests, the mud flats, the sides-of-roads which appeared so ideal for the dumping of bodies and trash. The landscaping job took me to the outskirts of the town, to all these kinds of places, and I missed Portland: Organized civic space, where you could walk to the store.

I had wanted my world to close around me, to protect me, and Olympia and my girlfriend there seemed like they could do that but they didn't. Instead I realized the community was like a bag over my head, a plastic one.

The four exits on I-5 took us south, towards Portland, out of the Puget Sound and into the hills, to the place we picked up the mowers every day. Lisha continued to talk to me in a familiar tone: "Me and my mom are super good friends, I mean I can tell her anything and she keeps me out of trouble. I mean she is the best friend I have, and not many people can say that about their moms. Like when I was nineteen, for my nineteenth birthday she took me to get a tattoo. It's of a dove and a red rose, a single, up on my left shoulder." Lisha pulled at her jacket so she could show me the tattoo, causing the truck to swerve.

I gripped the dashboard.

"I got another tattoo on the inside of my right ankle, the twins Castor and Polux, which are the sign for Gemini, because I'm a Gemini, and that symbolism is really important to me."

Lisha said that she was saving up to go to exotic animal training school. She wanted to work with big cats. She had experience with an exotic animal farm right down the road from where she grew up called *Ups and Downs Exotics*. They had pot-bellied pigs, ostriches, and llamas. She started working there when she was twelve, working for five dollars an hour under the table. She told me that she has a connection with animals.

The first job on the first day of landscaping was at a large house in a development outside of town. The tall windows of the house faced out toward the Puget Sound. The air was damp and marine. As foggy as it got in Portland, it was never like this—salty, and blinding white. The large lawn, pocked with moss, stretched to the woods on one side. We unloaded the mowers, the edgers, the rakes and the barrels. Lisha showed me how to gas up, how to pull out the choke to get the mower started.

The owner of the house came out, and Lisha called to him: "Hey we're just the mow crew, we're just here to mow the lawn. Guess you've never seen an all female mow crew, but we're not mowin' naked if that's what you were interested in!"

It was thirty-five degrees, there was still frost on the lawn.

The guy shrugged, embarrassed that there were even people there at all to do cold work. From time to time I looked in and could see he was watching a movie. I saw the shadow of another person in the house. These people had left dog shit in the yard for us to mow over. According to Lisha this was very unsanitary and there's no quicker way to spread disease.

After I quit the landscaping job, later that spring, I had to earn money by working at a heavy machinery auction. I was still in Olympia, it was April. I worked inside in the office where men from all over the South Sound area stood in lines waiting to hand over $43,000 in cash for a backhoe or dumptruck. Those were long days inside, uncut by natural light. We worked from five in the morning until ten at night, four days straight.

On one of my breaks I walked into the hall where they

drove the machines and trucks across a stage so that the men could bid on them. I ordered a hamburger and curly fries and sat watching the trucks. I saw Lisha driving a dumptruck across the stage. She was a big girl, and she looked small and very happy in the cab of the truck. She was waving to all the men bidding on the truck, flirting and saying things like, "Hiya, handsome!"

She must have had the day off landscaping. She lived close by Richie Brothers Heavy Machine Auction and I remember that once she told me she had been working there for a bunch of years since she was fourteen. She told me they paid her $150 under the table to drive those trucks all day. She could handle them, she said, even though the guys thought she couldn't.

The winter I worked with her, Lisha talked to me the whole time. She didn't seem to notice that I never spoke to her, except to signal my assent, or to ask her the question she had made obvious she would like to be asked:

"I was really young when I first smoked pot," she would say.

"How young?" I would ask.

She seemed to voice any thought that came into her head. Silence was awkward for her and she was trying to be friends with me in the only way she knew: Pure revelation.

I would sit back with my head bumping against the broken springs of the seat and close my eyes. Lisha continued to talk. She would talk about the job we had just done, or the one we were about to do, or the relative merits of electric- versus gas-powered tools. Lisha would talk about her hot date for the evening.

When I first met Lisha I thought she was a lesbian. I guess because I had referred to the company for so long as the "lesbian landscapers" I just assumed. She told me about a bar,

El Cantina, where they were "real accepting," and this made me think it even more. It took only two days to get it all out of her.

She and her girlfriend Angela had moved into a part of Tumwater that they called the Pit.

They called it that because there used to be a dry cleaner who would spill all their dirty polluted water down the blackberry-covered hill and it would get all in the groundwater. Everyone there was always sick from the pollution. Lisha said she got a girlfriend because she was sick of guys. She thought girls would be better for some reason, "you know, because girls are nicer and know what girls need in terms of emotionally and all. Not true."

Lisha said: "Angela was a total user bitch who used me and my friends and her family for everything. And she was a pot head. She still owes me like six hundred dollars and you know I'm never going to see that six hundred dollars ever again, that's a fact. And it's not like women are somehow better at your emotional needs and all than men. At least that's not my experience."

I thought, *yes*, but didn't say anything.

Lisha said: "We lived next to these Filipinos in the Pit and they were always making tons of noise, and just partying all the time. We used to yell at them because they made so much noise, but by the end it was us who was making all the noise because we were yelling and fighting so much. I mean, it's not like you start to go out with a girl and you don't fight. I seriously thought it was going to be so different from when you go out with guys. Because with guys you always fight, you kind of expect it, but with girls, you think it's not going to be that way. Well, like I said, Angela was one of the biggest users you have ever seen."

She said: "It got to be where I was the only one in the house who was working. It was me and Angela, and Angela's best friend and her sister. I was doing landscaping and then on the weekends I was working at the Texaco at the Taco Bell Express down there, that is until I mouthed off to the manager and got fired. But I was the only one with money, and they would be all like, *Lisha, can you go get us some groceries?* and I would. They were all users. My mom kept saying, *just detach*, but it wasn't that easy. Eventually I started fooling around with Jet, who is my boyfriend now, and then just kind of moved out back into my mom's house for a while and then to my new apartment that I got now."

Maybe a minute would pass, us, in silence.

I would get home from landscaping and talk on and on to my girlfriend about Lisha. About the Pit, El Cantina. About the lawns, and then the caked grass stuck in the mowers. I tried to tell her the stories like they were an adventure. I tried to tell them in the animated way Lisha had told them to me, with the same energy, the same excitedness, the same passion. But my girlfriend always looked away from me when I told her these stories. Eventually she hauled the television up from the basement and started watching it every night. If there wasn't anything on she'd watch the news, in Spanish.

I moved back to Portland.

By summer, she had started using the riding mower again. The grass grew fast on her acre.

Not Following the Rules
Christa Orth

I slid the proposal across the oak veneer conference table, my pleather chair squeaking as I reached. The University of Oregon president had sent his slimy lawyer to the union contract negotiations that day. He was the first to comment on our demands. "If we have to give protections to transsexuals, we'll have to give them to everyone—even Satanists."

At this point, we'd been arguing with the university for non-discrimination for transgender workers, along with salary and benefits raises, for four months. We were graduate students who slaved away for the university, teaching seventy-five percent of the course load, and we deserved a raise—and respect. I'd introduced the transgender protections as a bargaining point, having learned at a queer labor conference that trans workers struggled with discrimination and that they weren't protected under most labor contracts, let alone federal law. Queers and allies on the campus rallied around the issue. We consulted lawyers at the National Center for Lesbian Rights. And we brought our simple, justified request to the university administration.

Comparing trans folks to Satanists was ridiculous, but I was most angry that the university lawyer was dismissing the need to protect gender minorities. Other objections came from across the table. The human resources lady claimed that sexual harassment law would protect transsexuals at work. The dean of the college asked if we could prove that there were transgender workers who had already experienced discrimination on our campus. We explained that transgender case law showed that discrimination was difficult to fight based on sex or sexism. We explained that we did not yet know of any discrimination at our school, but we had compiled hundreds of pages of cases of injustice from around the country. We were trying to protect transgender workers before they were discriminated against.

One day, during a particularly grueling bargaining session, we broke to caucus about the third meager salary proposal the university had shoved at us. We were on the ninth floor of a gray industrial building. I found my perch on a windowsill overlooking the quad. I looked down to the street below. Someone had chalked a message so large a crowd had gathered around it: "I am a transgender worker. I exist." This was the sign of resistance and solidarity I needed to keep up the fight.

I did research for two years in grad school about the history of the queer workers rights movement in the Pacific Northwest—as much to fill a gap in the historical record as to find out where I'd come from. Most of my friends, even the queer ones, never learned about queer history in school and really don't know much about it. We picture the old-school femme in her woolen pencil skirt and the butch of her dreams decked out in a pressed men's suit, complete with favorite tie and felt fedora, but the first thing I learned about queer history was that the butches and femmes of the 1940s and '50s dressed hyper-masculine or feminine to pass as heterosexual couples and to secretly signal each other in bars.

Psychologists considered homosexuality, transvestisism, and transsexuality mental disorders. Doctors treated these disorders in mental institutions with medication and shock therapies. The judicial system criminalized homosexuality and crossdressing. Police arrested people for having same-sex affairs or for dressing as the "wrong" gender. Employers could fire someone if there was even a rumor they were queer. Schools taught that homosexuals were dangerous pedophiles. Many queers had to stay in the closet at work, especially if they were teachers. Right-wing conservatism fueled anti-gay politics, and ballot measures threatened to prevent gay rights. HIV/AIDS killed thousands of gay men in the 1980s and 1990s, while the Reagan and Bush administrations refused to do anything about it. Queer communities were profoundly affected, and whole groups of friends died.

Through it all, people resisted homophobia and transphobia by fighting back. And they resisted in the simplest way—by being themselves. As a thirty-ish queer labor activist and teacher, I got interested in discovering how queers before me lived their daily lives, so I started asking queer elders about the places most of them had to go everyday: work. The stories my elders told me make me feel more connected to queer history, because just like me, my elders found creative ways to resist conformity. My queer history education came from learning about the daily struggles and triumphs of radical folks who didn't want to follow the rules.

The year was 1973, and Steve Harmon was plugged into a switchboard in a downtown building on SW 4th Avenue and Oak. His late shift had just begun. The clock struck 9 p.m., the bewitching hour. Steve answered the line, "Pacific Northwest Bell Directory Assistance—How may I help you?" The man on the other end breathed heavily for a moment, then asked for the number for The Rip Tide. Steve had never been there, but he knew The Rip Tide was a gay bar. He gave the man the number quickly, he knew it by heart. The man paused for a few moments, then asked suggestively, "Going out tonight?"

Steve had never had that kind of obvious proposition at work before. He had worked at the Multnomah County Central Library for a couple of years reshelving books in the stacks. His first lover, Jeff, got him the job. Steve didn't realize it at first, but almost everyone who worked at the library was gay or lesbian. It was the late 1960s, and almost no one was really "out," but Steve slowly learned that he was working among people just like him. He knew a gay man at the library who had been with his partner for twenty years. He went to a party at a co-worker's house full of gay people. The man who interviewed him for the library job, Jerry, always hired either gay boys or cute boys. Known as "the queen of the stacks," he wore a ruby ring and flirted with everyone. No one really talked about being gay at the library, but Steve felt right at home. He'd been out since he was a young boy, but the library was the first place he was immersed in queer culture.

Steve felt both lucky and unlucky to come out so early—before the gay liberation movement began to change attitudes about homosexuality. In 1965, when Steve was thirteen, he fell in lust with a hunky neighbor—a twenty-eight-year-old straight guy. He didn't realize at the time that pursuing an older man would be dangerous. He just had a major crush on this absolutely gorgeous guy. He wrote a couple of anonymous love notes to the neighbor, telling him he thought he was cute and that he wanted to go out with him. He snuck down the street and put them in the neighbor's mailbox.

The notes were fairly innocent, but the neighbor got creeped out and, not wanting to be implicated in a pedophilic homosexual affair, he turned the notes over to the police. The search began for the anonymous author. The only things Steve revealed about himself was that he was a thirteen-year-old boy. The police hired a handwriting expert who surveyed handwriting samples of all the thirteen-year-old boys at Franklin and Cleveland high schools. That's how they found him.

A few weeks after Steve delivered the note declaring his unrequited love, two men in overcoats showed up at his house. Steve knew immediately that they were police officers, and why they were there. Just as they flashed their badges, Steve's mom came screaming into the house from work, assuming that Steve's delinquent older brother had gotten into trouble again. "It's not about Gary," the officers told her. "It's about Steve." Her jaw dropped. But Steve's mom soon learned about the secret notes, the handwriting expert, and her son's homosexuality. Steve had apparently broken a number of laws, including sending obscene material through the mail. By this time, Steve was so scared, he was quaking. Still, he protested—the notes weren't obscene and he hadn't sent them through the mail. He'd hand delivered them!

The police could have arrested Steve right then and taken him to juvenile hall. But they made a deal that his parents would take him to court sometime later for a hearing. When the police left, his mother wondered out loud what had made Steve homosexual. She blamed herself. Steve felt that he'd just always liked boys. He was just unlucky that he got caught.

After a couple of months, Steve assumed things had blown over, but one afternoon, he and his mom went for a drive down Burnside Street to Gresham, and to a beautiful campus with big lawns. The signs out front read "Morningside Hospital." Steve had not been privy to the judge's decision in his case—the only way he could stay out of juvie was to undergo psychiatric care. Steve's mom's employer, Tektronix, had offered to pay for his treatment at Morningside. He felt scared again. He'd obviously done something terribly wrong.

The other folks in Ward A included a fifteen-year-old boy who set things on fire, a woman who had tried to kill her children, and a boy who sniffed glue. The glue-sniffer, Steve noticed, was also totally gorgeous. As Steve waited, he got more and more anxious. No one told him he would be coming to a place like this.

Finally, Steve was called into the office of Dr. James Kraus. "Do you know why you're here?" the doctor asked him.

Steve thought carefully. He knew what he said next could have grave consequences. He gathered up all his thirteen-year-old courage and said, "Because I'm a homosexual."

Then a remarkable thing happened. Instead of the doctor telling Steve about the abnormalities of homosexuality, Dr. Kraus said simply, "we can't change you, you are who you are. But I'd like to talk to about this."

Steve was relieved.

The doctor asked him to stay overnight in the hospital for some tests and Steve agreed. Maybe he'd get a chance to flirt with the gorgeous glue-sniffer.

Five days of tests, group therapy, and individual sessions with Dr. Kraus went by. Steve's aunt and uncle came for a visit. His parents had told them that Steve had a nervous breakdown. They wanted to take him out for a picnic, but the hospital wouldn't let Steve go—he'd been committed for being a homosexual. He stayed at Morningside Hospital for thirty-one days. Steve went through many things that would scare any child, including witnessing the effects of shock therapy on the woman who had tried to kill her children, but his experience at the hospital was surprisingly positive. Dr. Kraus helped Steve learn how to incorporate his gayness into his daily life, and he saw him for weekly sessions for four more years. Steve learned how to be himself. In an age of horror stories of homosexuals forced into mental institutions, Steve felt lucky that his parents had found him an enlightened psychologist.

Steve never went into the closet as a gay man. He developed a community of queers during his teenage years. Most of his friends at Franklin High School were gay. His boyfriend, Jeff, got him the job at the Central Library. Steve had never really been immersed in a straight world, but when he left the library and started his new job, he was surrounded by straight folks and women.

When Pacific Northwest Bell hired Steve in 1973, he became the first male phone operator in Portland. His sister got him the job as soon as the phone company started hiring men. The company had also started to hire women as linemen. So here Steve was, sitting in rows of women, answering the directory assistance calls. And his was the only male voice on the phones.

The directory assistance operators had to be plugged in to their board at all times on their shift. Pacific Northwest Bell valued customer service, and timed each call. Callers were never to wait more than fifteen seconds for the number they were requesting. The operators sat with a big Portland General Directory in front of them. They wore rubber finger condoms to flip the pages faster. There was a red button on the right hand side of the switchboard that you used to disconnect calls. But you were never supposed to push that red button unless someone was obscene or threatening.

During his first week answering directory assistance, Steve got several deep breathers on the line. When he answered, the callers would pause, not say anything, and then hang up. One day, Steve answered and a guy started screaming, "Oh my god! Get a haircut and get a man's job!" Steve had short hair, but the caller had obviously expected to hear a woman's voice.

Hostile callers continued to verbally abuse Steve. If you were a man doing a woman's job, you had to be gay. A number of people called Steve "queer" or "faggot." One caller talked about Jesus. Steve's supervisor, Christine, called him off the board one day for a private meeting. She'd listened in on one of the hostile calls. She hoped Steve was taking it all in stride—the callers just weren't used to a man's voice. Steve was embarrassed that his presence was causing so much havoc, but he felt it was important for Christine to know that it hurt when the callers called him a faggot. Steve's cheeks burned. He took a deep breath. "I want you to know I'm gay," he told Christine. It was the first time he'd ever come out at work. Christine was supportive. She told him if he ever got a hostile caller not to argue with them, not to take their abuse, but just click them off. Steve didn't feel embarrassed anymore. Callers were just going to have to get used to his voice. The next time a caller called him a faggot, Steve didn't hesitate. He pressed the red button. Click.

Steve found other people like him at Pacific Northwest Bell. He made fast friends with Lynn, another operator, a "sissy butch." She never wore a dress, never wore a bra, and dated femme women. Steve and Lynn sat across from each other. On slow shifts, they chatted and played around. Lynn took Steve out to a women's bar under the bridges in Southeast. The first time they walked in together, the women tried to kick him out. Lynn had to vouch that he was gay.

There were other gay fixtures at the phone company. In the name of good customer service, each week the company published a new updated directory for the operators to flip through. Each alphabetic section was divided by a neatly organized list of frequently-called phone numbers. Every gay bar in Portland was on the frequently-called list. Around nine o'clock, directory assistance was flooded with calls for the smoky, sexy bars like Dema's Tavern (now Darcelle XV), The Tav, The Half Moon, and The Rip Tide. Pretty soon, Steve had memorized them all. When Steve answered the line, he wasn't allowed to have open conversations with the callers. But that didn't stop gay men from asking, "Going out tonight?" And that didn't stop Steve from telling them his own coded line: "I'm not old enough."

Almost twenty years later in Wilsonville, Pat Young looked out across a sea of gray cubicles, the old orange office chairs popping out like sore thumbs adjacent the row of shiny new conference rooms. She was on her tip toes, trying to quietly balance as she peeked over the wall. Her tall friend Don just stood, waiting. Soon, in the fluorescent light, she spotted one—a muscular forty-something man in a turtleneck shirt, vest, and pleated khaki pants. "There goes one!" she whispered.

"No, no, I thought that guy was gay but no," the tall man whispered back.

Pat wanted to sink down to rest her feet, but she was determined to find just one more. She clutched the letter, signed by the requisite fourteen Tektronix employees. All she needed was one more signature before she could turn it in to Human Resources.

Pat Young's story is about a gem in the heart of corporate America. She worked as a technical writer for the Oregon company Tektronix for fifteen years in the 1980s and '90s. She wasn't cut out for corporate culture—she hated the "rat maze of cubicles," and the "rah rah" motivational speeches. But she made a good living. Coming out as a lesbian at work was one of the ways she resisted the gloom of her workplace. Pat's story is about the misery of working for a corporation, but also about the power of resistance.

Pat had initially inquired about domestic partner benefits, and had been told through countless voicemails, emails, and meetings, that it was just a matter of time before Tek employees would get them. At the last pass, the HR manager guy had told her to write a letter asking for benefits for same-sex couples and to get fifteen gay people to sign it in support—either with their full names or initials. Pat didn't know even a few gay people at Tek. It wasn't a very gay-friendly environment. It wasn't blatantly homophobic—although a few managers made anti-gay jokes—but no one was out at Tek. When Pat saw her straight co-workers decorate their cubicles with wedding or honeymoon photos, she knew she wouldn't be doing that. She decorated with tear-outs from Arizona Highways and her bowling scores. It was 1991.

Still, Pat set out to find her fifteen gays—she was determined to submit the letter and to get benefits as soon as possible. Pat had a girlfriend who couldn't hold down a job, and she was continually losing her health insurance. Pat knew that one of her straight co-workers' wife had lost her job, and he was able to cover her under his insurance. She wanted that security for her and her girlfriend, too. She'd read in the *New York Times* that big high tech companies like Lotus Corporation had given their employees domestic partner benefits. She was sure that all she needed to do was convince Tek that there was a need, and give them a template.

Pat picked her first target. He was a guy she saw when she'd go get tea on her breaks. He was about her height, five-foot-four, with a big thick handlebar mustache. If anyone looked gay it was this guy. She asked him to sit with her in the cafeteria and she explained about the domestic partner benefits and the letter. He just looked at her. "I'm not gay."

Oh shit.

And then he said, "Well, how's it going?"

Not very well, Pat admitted. She wasn't worried about this guy, but Pat started getting paranoid that if she just went around using her faulty gaydar, she might offend someone and she might get in trouble. She decided to go a different route.

She went to a lesbian brunch one weekend, hoping to find someone who knew some lesbians at Tektronics—it was the largest high tech corporation in Oregon, after all. She got one name from that endeavor—Bobbi.

Bobbi worked at Tek in Beaverton, so Pat made the drive. They met and talked, but Bobbi was close to retirement and didn't want to risk her pension. She declined. But she gave Pat the name of a guy who worked in Wilsonville. This guy worked just a few cubicles down from Pat, but she had no idea he was gay. He was the first one to sign her letter. She made a photocopy of it and kept the copy safe at home. No corporate shredder was going to get a hold of her precious signature.

He knew a gay couple that worked at Tek, but they didn't want to meet at work, so Pat drove to their house on Macadam to get their signatures. They knew one other guy, and so on. Pat followed every lead she got, driving back and forth between Wilsonville and Beaverton, meeting people in "safe" locations or after hours. She met one guy who initially refused to sign because he managed Tek accounts in South America and he thought that if people found out he was gay in South America, it would be bad for business. But, eventually, he came around. She met one guy, Jose, who took her into a private conference room to sign the letter, and then broke down and told her he had AIDS. He was so scared of people finding out at work—at the time, there was little to no education about AIDS or how it was contracted. Pat was taken aback. She didn't know what to do. Gays at Tek really had nowhere to turn.

After two months of looking for folks to sign the letter, and after exhausting all her contacts for signers, Pat went back to Bobbi, the woman who had declined to sign because of her retirement. This time she was able to convince Bobbi to sign. Pat took the letter and photocopied it to send off to the head of benefits, Ed Nieubuurt. Pat had written in the letter that the company motto of Tektronix was "Enabling Innovation." She wrote that Tektronix touted that the company treated its employees well, and hopefully that treatment applied to gay employees as well as heterosexual employees. Now was the perfect time for Tektronix to be a leader and extend health benefits to the partners of its gay employees. Finally, Pat wrote that she was pleased that all fifteen people had decided to sign the letter rather than initial it. Pat hand-delivered the letter.

Pat noted all the communication she had up until then about the domestic partner benefits in a typed log which she kept at home. She checked in with Ed after a month and he was impressed by the number of people who signed full names. She checked in with him in another month and he reported he'd sent it to his boss, and that his boss had sent it back to him with a note that said "What do you think?" Pat waited two months this time before she checked in. Ed hadn't had the time to make the proposal to his boss, he said. But he hadn't forgotten them. It was 1992.

The Oregon Citizens Alliance, the statewide anti-gay political group, had opened up shop near the Wilsonville Tektronix. They had filed ballot Measure 9, which would have made it legal to fire gays and lesbians, and illegal to mention homosexuality or anything about HIV/AIDS in schools. Another of the OCA's anti-gay measures had passed four years earlier. The only thing Pat heard about that vote was from one of her straight co-workers who, the morning after it passed, acknowledged, "last night was a bad night for you." There wasn't much campaigning for or against this new Measure 9 at Tek. There were a couple of gay-friendly "No on 9" bumper stickers in the parking lot, but on election Tuesday, the anticipation about the vote was palpable, and Pat didn't do any work. She just sought out other gay people and hung out with them by their cubicles, just waiting. When Measure 9 was defeated, gay and straight co-workers congratulated each other. This time, people cared.

Meanwhile, PJ Kleffner, who worked on the South America accounts, had come out at work and started a Tek Gay and Lesbian Employees group. Pat joined. She updated them at each meeting about her progress with the benefits bureaucracy. The group sent their announcement to TekWeek, their employee newsletter. The editor of the newsletter balked at the announcement and asked them "What if every group runs an ad?" Eventually, the ad appeared, and Pat was being called into the conference room like a child in trouble. Apparently some employees had trouble with the ads. In addition, they weren't to use a company phone number to advertise their group. This was discrimination, Pat thought. No one would have made complaints about any of the other employee groups. Pat had several meetings with the editor just to get him to run the ads. He always had an excuse, saying groups had to have an agenda item printed in their ad, or the printer must have left it out. Pat went all the way to some vice president who confirmed it was OK to advertise the Gay and Lesbian Employee Group in the company newsletter. The editor of TekWeek reluctantly ran the ads, but sporadically. A guy in the Gay and Lesbian Employee Group had a special phone line put into his house for the group to use.

It was like learning how to follow the rules all over again. There were signs up everywhere that also advertised so and so's kid's basketball tournament, or the company picnic. The Gay and Lesbian group put signs up to advertise their meetings and updates on the domestic partner benefits. Their signs would go up, and then they would be mysteriously down. Pretty soon, Pat was being called into a conference room again. This time, it was that the group had violated several Tek policies.

You were only allowed to post signs on designated employee bulletin boards. The boards were not marked and different in each building, but they were listed in the employee handbook. The signs could only be posted for one month. Pat and the group agreed to follow the rules. They designated a guy named Bill to be the sign poster. But some rogue then made copies of the group's signs and put them on everyone's desk. Gasp! The top agenda item of each Tektronix Gay and Lesbian Employee Group meeting was always about the struggle of advertising their group so the gays and lesbians could find each other.

Pat continued to diligently check in with the higher-ups about the benefits. She had begun to send them packets of information from other high tech companies like Lotus and Apple that were starting to provide domestic partner benefits for same-sex couples. Ed Nieubuurt left Pat a voicemail that he would check in with Lotus. Pat had joined Rights for Domestic Partners Coalition, a Portland group of city, county, and library workers run by Chris Tanner, who eventually sued Oregon Health and Sciences University and won in 1998. Ed had told Pat that Tek needed more information about what the actual costs of these benefits would be for the company. So Pat sent along the extensive research that the coalition group had done about these costs—they were nominal. Pat had a meeting with Ed who said he would put together a statement about why Tek should provide domestic partner benefits and that he would call Kaiser and Good Health insurance companies to make sure they would go along.

Two months later, Ed told Pat he was leaving Tek. But he was still working on the proposal, and in light of the fact that Apple provided these benefits, he was confident that Tek would follow suit. A month later, Pat saw Ed out at lunch. He was already in his new job. He'd passed the information on to his replacement. He suggested Pat contact her. It was 1993.

Pat voicemailed back and forth with the benefits department. Ed's replacement was also planning to leave Tek. She called a vice president to see who she could follow up with. His admin person said he would be out for the next eight months. Someone tipped Pat off that Tektronix had hired a workforce diversity manager named Catrinus Wallet, and she set up a meeting with him to explain how she had submitted the letter of support from fifteen employees over two years earlier and was still waiting for an answer. Catrinus said this was something he would work on, but first he needed a couple of months to finish writing the Tektronix Diversity Mission Statement.

Pat insisted on a face-to-face meeting with another HR benefits person, Terri, who requested more information. Pat dropped off a thick notebook of her two-year log of voicemails, emails and meetings over this issue, cost benefit analysis, other high tech company's policies, insurance information, and glowing newspaper articles about how Apple and Lotus were offering benefits to same-sex couples. Terri set up a meeting with Pat and another higher-up, David. Pat was tired and didn't say much in the meeting. She just watched and listened. David wanted to show the notebook to Tim and Karen, yet more benefits people. He said he would have a yes or no answer for Pat in six months—by July. He informed her that the letter of support signed by fifteen employees hadn't been necessary. He wanted the letter found and shredded. It was 1994.

After hundreds of emails, voicemails, and meetings that went nowhere, Pat was tired and frustrated. By this time, she had become a middle-manager, and was dealing with a lot of crap like trying to get her female employees equal pay for equal work. Her friend died of cancer. And her girlfriend had left her. Pat didn't want to tell anybody about her break-up for fear they would ask if she didn't have a domestic partner, why would she want or need benefits? In the spring of 1994, she saw David Franks and he said that things looked pretty good for domestic partner benefits. Five percent of people who had responded to the employee survey mentioned something about them. She met with Catrinus the diversity guy and he said it looked like it was a go. Tektronix was getting ready to "roll out" a new and exciting employee benefits package, and Pat thought, well this is it, all my hard work is finally coming to something.

In August 1994, Pat passed by David Franks on her tea break. "Well did you hear the news? It's not going to happen." Pat was crushed. She went back to her gray cubicle and cried. There were fancy color-copied fliers posted all over the office about the new and improved employee benefits package. And Pat knew she was one of the many employees that would sit through the "rah rah" roll out meeting and be excluded. From the letter that went nowhere, to the promises that managers and VP's had made to her over four years, finally she knew. It wasn't going to happen.

That same month, Pat's name was randomly drawn for a very special benefit for a group of employees. It was a surprise lunch with the vice presidents. Pat felt it was their misfortune that they had chosen her because she was going to give them an earful. During lunch, the VPs asked the employees which divisions they worked in and thanked them for their dedication to Tektronix. They asked if anyone had any questions. Pat wanted to know what happened with the benefits. With her voice shaking, Pat told the VPs that people had assured her that domestic partner benefits would be included. What happened? The two VPs, Carl Neun and John Karalis, said the Tektronix Policy Council had made the decision. Pat was clutching a Tektronix diversity brochure and asked why the company felt they could discriminate against gays and lesbians. The VPs kept saying "they blah blah blah" and Pat kept asking "who is they?" An HR lady in the room was getting upset that Pat was upset, but Pat kept asking them, following them into the hallway after the lunch had ended. The HR lady tried to calm Pat down by promising her a meeting with the head of HR to explain what had happened.

In that meeting, Pat found out that the "they" on the policy council had actually been the two VPs she had been having lunch with. Well, she finally made it to the top and spoke her mind unabashedly to the very executives that were discriminating against gays and lesbians at Tektronix.

Homophobia and transphobia spans decades in Portland, and it's certainly not over. But I was surprised and inspired by the ways that Steve and Pat overcame daily homophobia to live their lives on their own terms. And their resistance paid off.

Tektronics paid for Pat to go back to school at Portland State University. She started part time, then quit working and wrote her Master's thesis on homophobia and Ballot Measure 9. And she met her new girlfriend at Tek—Fern, from Human Resources. Steve got a job at Portland State, and joined the effort to protect LGBTQ students, staff, and faculty from discrimination. He was also one of the early HIV/AIDS activists, and ensured that his workplace didn't succumb to AIDS hysteria. As for me, my graduate student bargaining team finally won transgender protections in our contract in 2002—we were one of the first in the United States.

In an age when the media threatens to paint queers as caricatures, our real and lived stories help remind us how to resist conformity. Queer history teaches us that we aren't destined to follow the rules.

Directory Assistance
Nicole Vaicunas

Lesley and I had no supervision on the graveyard shift. We took advantage of it, too. We raced our chairs up and down the hallways and around the cubes. We took turns napping. We ate at our cubes, which was forbidden because at some point someone had spilled their food and never cleaned their work area. This led to an army of ants invading the call center. We weren't doing anything important, like healing the sick or running the free world. We were phone jockeys.

We provided information—or "directory assistance"—to cell phone users. They'd dial 4-1-1 and get our prerecorded greeting. "Thank you for calling information, my name is such and such, may I have your city and listing please?" They'd rattle off whatever listing they needed, and we'd search an outdated database to give them the number and connect them to their listing. Sometimes they'd want movie times. If they were lost or needed help finding their destination, we gave them driving directions. This was tricky if they lived in Pocatello.

Rumors had been swirling about one of the guys on the day shift. He'd told Colleen she had great breasts. According to the rumor mill, there were other complaints against him. So, in a brilliant move by management, they planned to move him to the graveyard shift with Lesley and I. His name was Lewis. He smelled like cat piss, testosterone, and Old Spice. He wore T-shirts that pictured wolves, eagles, wizards, or the American flag. The shirt was usually tucked into pants two sizes too small, held up by a brown belt with a golden buckle the size of a toddler's head. The ensemble was not complete without his camouflage jacket and matching duffle bag.

For the first week of his shift, Lewis sat away from us. He said nothing, despite our attempts to welcome him. He carried his duffle bag everywhere. We spent hours plotting ways to figure out the contents of the mysterious camouflage bag. I wanted to know what was in there but not nearly as much as Lesley did. She was nosy enough for the two of us. "I'll bet there are human heads in it," Lesley whispered.

I was surprised when Lewis opted to sit by me one evening. We chatted between calls. I learned that he was a veteran. Apparently, he served in Operation Desert Storm. Or at least he was in the service at the time. He was in Germany working on a "super secretive mission" which may or may not have been related to the Gulf War. He may or may not have been in Kuwait. He may or may not have met Norman Schwartzkopf. Lewis wouldn't clarify because everything was "super secretive." When I told him to stop calling everything "super secretive" and say "classified" instead, he quit talking to me all together except when he needed help finding the number for Sassy's— the strip club in southeast, *not* the cab company.

In those days, I kept a picture of a baby penguin in my wallet with my ID, debit card, and bus pass. There was something about the tiny, fuzzy beast that made me happy. It squashed bad thoughts and unhappy feelings with the sheer power of its cuteness. It was only fair to share my prized posession with my new co-worker. Perhaps Lewis would find comfort and some joy in the baby bird in my wallet. Perhaps we would have a common bond over this silly picture. But when I showed him the picture, Lewis screamed like a child being confronted with the realization that his next door neighbor really *does* eat children. After three more attempts to show him the picture (one with an accompanying high pitched, demonic voice), I put the picture away.

"Were your parents eaten by penguins?" I asked him. "I get that you're afraid of penguins. I don't understand why."

"I am not afraid of penguins," Lewis snapped.

"I mean, if it makes any difference, my girlfriend is afraid of penguins, too," I lied. My girlfriend at the time was afraid of her hallucinations and the voices in her head, not penguins, but I was trying to make him feel better.

"Girlfriend?"

"Yes, *girlfriend.* You have had one of those, correct?"

"I've had *many.*" His eyes narrowed as he turned away.

"Well, I have one."

"That's disgusting," he said to his monitor. "It's unnatural."

"How in the hell is it *unnatural?*"

"Women need men. We have baby batter and we're stronger and better. It's a fact. You need us. You couldn't survive without us." I didn't see the need to mention that my girlfriend had a husband. This wouldn't have been the right time. Besides, who was he to judge my relationship? He didn't know me. He didn't know her. I vowed not to say anything to him the rest of the night, even if he asked for help.

"Hey, I can't find the 'G' spot.' Can you help me?" he asked, flipping through the four main screens on our directory system.

"Of course you can't find it," I snickered. "Did you try the phone book?"

"What kind of business is it?" he asked. "I'm sorry sir, I'm trying to find it right now. We're looking in the phone book. Hello? Sir? Sir? Are you there?" Lewis turned to me. "He hung up. Maybe next time you can help me a little quicker?"

I resumed ignoring him.

Lewis seemed unaware of our hatred of him. I should clarify that Lesley didn't hate him, but felt he was too obnoxious not to teach a valuable lesson. I hated him and tormented him with stories about the madcap adventures of my bisexual friends. In return, Lewis fed us scrumptious personal morsels that we mentally devoured to use later. After learning that he frequented many Internet dating sites, we rushed out and created free profiles on some of them. Our favorite was a college co-ed we dreamed up. We named her Tina and she and Lewis hit it off instantly. To our dismay, he was quick to request a picture. We scoured the Internet and finally found a picture from a porn site. To our surprise, he printed it and brought it to work.

"Tina sent me a picture," he said.

Lesley was sitting in the cube between us.

I lowered my head so he wouldn't see me laughing.

"I think I really like her."

For a moment, a nanosecond, I almost felt bad, but then I remembered how this whole thing had started.

Lewis opened his duffle bag and pulled out a picture. Sure enough, it was the same "college girl." Tina was standing in a dorm type room, wearing a white sweater with a giant red P on the left side of the chest. The banner on the wall said "Penn State." We were screwed. "I don't think this is a real picture, though," he said. "She looks familiar to me, but I can't place her." We were definitely screwed.

"I wouldn't sweat it," I yawned. "Even if it isn't real, do you like her anyway?"

"I don't like liars," Lewis snapped. "Sending me a fake picture is lying."

"What if she has body image issues?"

"Why would she have body issues? Oh, because women have body issues. I'm betting she's the size of a whale."

"For the record, not all of us have body image issues," I corrected him. "Do you carry a scale around with you? An intake chart? 'Sorry miss, you're weighing in at two hundred pounds. My weight limit is one thirty-five! Come see me again when you've lost that sixty-five. Oh hell, for you, we can start talking when you're down by forty-five.' Whatever, Lewis."

"Take that back! I do not carry an intake form and my weight limit isn't one thirty-five. It's one-seventy."

"You have a weight limit?" Lesley raised an eyebrow. "No offense Lewis, but you're not someone who should have a weight limit."

"What's that supposed to mean?"

"What I mean is, maybe you should wear a T-shirt that actually fits you," Lesley shrugged.

Lewis and Tina shared personal tidbits and a common love of hunting and Jesus. Tina liked hunting because her dead father had taken her hunting once. She couldn't join the military because of a bad leg from a car accident that killed her brother. We told him about the time she was almost molested at church camp when she was eleven. The whole episode made her feel self-conscious and she needed therapy.

A week later, a day shift supervisor smelled something odd in one of the cubes. People had complained about the smell and the stickiness. The odor eventually wore off, but the stickiness remained. Later, in a midnight confession, Lewis sheepishly admitted that he had jacked off in that very cube. In addition to the stench and stickiness, there was a stained office chair.

Lesley gagged when I told her. But she had more dirt. "I didn't want to tell you this, but he's a spy," she explained. "Marcy doesn't trust us. He's been staying up to an hour after each shift, sitting in Marcy's office. I'm coming in tomorrow after your shift and I'm talking with her. Oh, by the way. Sending him an email with Tina's real picture."

By the time we went to speak to our useless manager, Marcy, she had forms already drafted up for us to sign. "I can't tell you what will happen, but I need you to sign this."

"How can you make us sign something when we didn't really do anything wrong?" I asked. "We didn't encourage it."

"But you behaved inappropriately," she said. Behaved inappropriately? Was she serious?

"We weren't the ones who masturbated at work. He left *stains*, Marcy. *Stains*. Check the chair." Marcy stared at me. "Look, I'm not sure what you *think* we did, but whatever it is, we didn't do it. You stuck that jackass on our shift with no supervisor. How many complaints did he have against him when the shift change went through?"

"Sign the form and get out." Marcy pointed at the door.

And that's what we did.

On my way out, Lewis glared at me. I could tell he wanted to add me to his super secret collection of heads. Fortunately, he'd never have the chance.

Back home, I checked my email. One new message from Lesley. *Subject: The Real Tina.* The picture was Lewis's head pasted on the body of a penguin. Lesley had painted on a hot pink eye patch and yellow curls bright enough to blind the sun.

THEN SOMETIMES THIS FEELING OF HOME

Bridges
Wayne Gregory

I had often crossed bridges in Portland. Across the Burnside Bridge, then down NE Sandy to cruise the dark, impersonal maze of the gay baths. Across the Broadway Bridge and onto SW 3rd to sit on a barstool and put dollar bills into a hunky male stripper's g-string. Across the other bridges—the Fremont Bridge, the Marquam Bridge, the Steel Bridge, the Morrison, the Hawthorne, and once even the Sauvie Island bridge for a one-time encounter with an anonymous man who went only by his screen name. Tonight as I crossed the Ross Island, I fumbled with the map, kept my eyes peeled for the 99E/Milwaukie exit.

For all my forty-eight years, I kept my sexual orientation hidden from even my most intimate friends and family. For just over two-thirds of that time, I'd kept it hidden from myself. The fundamentalist, Southern world where I grew up hardly acknowledged homosexuality and, when it did, condemned it. "You shall not lie with a man as with a woman, for that is an abomination before God," the ranting, thick-haired evangelists cried from their Old Testaments.

I understood my sexuality only as a sinful urge, like an alcoholic's weakness for drink. I imagined I could pray it away and by some miraculous act of God, it would pass. Sometimes I thought of it as a disease, a mental defect that could only be cured by time and more diligent efforts on my part. In my youth and the early years of my adult life, I simply couldn't accept the possibility that my out of place feelings and early, random encounters with men could be the expression of my being gay.

I turned onto 99E/Multnomah, scrutinized the signs for my exit. Unfamiliar territory. I was afraid I'd be late. The concert would begin in thirty minutes and I wasn't sure how far I had to go. *I can't believe I'm doing this*, I thought. The idea of a Christian concert for a mostly-gay audience by a singer I'd listened to in college seemed totally incongruous. Cynthia Clawson, a young, golden throated singer of Jesus songs back in the early '80s was singing today for a group of gay evangelicals holding a conference in the city. The first time I'd heard about the group, I was skeptical. The idea that gay and evangelical could somehow co-exist was difficult for me to get my head around. Two days earlier, I'd shown up for the conference and freaked when I saw my nametag on the table among all those queers. I ran out of the building, certain I couldn't handle this collision of worlds.

I had carefully constructed the kind of life expected of every young, Christian male of my generation: I got married, had children, took an active role in my church, and built a successful career—in my case, as a college professor. My fantasies and sexual experiences were anomalies, moments of backsliding and weakness for which I could repent, beg forgiveness, and then walk away from, confident they would never happen again.

But they did happen again. Over and over. More and more frequently. The older I got and the harder I tried, the more frequent and intense the suppressed passions and the greater the compulsion to act them out. I thought I might be possessed. Could I have the demons cast out of me? I'd seen it happen once, to some helpless boy at the holy roller church back home.

"I rebuke you, spirit of homosexuality, in the name of Jesus!" The preacher pushed his sweaty palm against the hot brow of the long-haired teenager with quivering lips. With his other hand raised toward heaven, the preacher pushed harder against the boy's head and yelled at the Devil in him: "I command you foul spirits to release this boy from his perversion and fill him with the Holy Ghost!"

The elders of the church surrounded the boy with outstretched hands, murmuring in strange tongues, ready to catch him when the demons left. Two of them lightly touched their hands to his back as the preacher pushed harder and railed in his own language of heaven: "Shambala killiala palabronda mantakalla." With a final push, the preacher cried out, "In Jesus' name, be gone!"

The teenager's body convulsed, then stiffened and fell backward like a cut tree. The praying elders led him to the floor and left him crying. Minutes later the boy stood up and gave testimony. He'd been delivered from the gay demons and was now as straight as any man there. Three weeks later, he was caught getting his cock sucked by the music minister in the back of the choir room. The demons had returned.

The same gay demons kept hounding me. *Why was the God in me powerless to set me free?* In time, I came to realize that this was no demon at all—just the cruel handiwork of a God who had created me to be something I didn't want to be. I would never change, no matter how hard I tried. With this realization, I slipped into despair. I swam like a snake at the bottom of a dark well. I did the best I could to maintain my façade and cling to the life I'd made. So convincing was the lie that sometimes I felt almost happy. But I couldn't keep it at bay. My despair threatened to swallow me.

Portland became my place to escape and explore the real gay boy inside me. I crossed over from my world of manufactured straightness onto a shore where the hidden expressions of who I was could flourish. I wanted to believe these indulgences were counter to who I really was, or wanted to be. The fog of shame and guilt I lived in kept me from seeing that in these moments of seeming darkness, I was actually closest to finding my clarity.

I turned onto the Eastmoreland/Reed College exit, and took a left on SE Bybee Boulevard, eventually veering left onto SE 28th Avenue and driving alongside the Eastmoreland Golf course. The late afternoon July sky felt soft and lazy like a baby blue blanket draped over my shoulders. The air blew cool through the car windows, with just a trace of the heat from earlier in the day riding underneath it. It reminded me of the day a year earlier when I had been forced to come out to my wife of nearly twenty-five years. We sat on the patio under the shade of the pear trees.

"Are you gay?" Her voice was deliberate, but gentle; her face almost hopeful, as if the answer to years of frustration and self-doubt was finally at hand.

"Why would you ask that?"

She touched my arm sympathetically. "I found the picture and the email."

I knew the ones she meant. An email setting up a random tryst with MuscleguyPDX, a man I'd met online, accompanied by an indiscreet picture of myself. I didn't even know the guy's real name and would never see him again. I stared ahead, paralyzed, as the world I had carefully and painstakingly built crumbled beneath the weight of its own dishonesty. Almost fifty years. Almost fifty years I had kept the lie together, hoping it would die its own fading death one day, only to have it end in this abrupt moment beneath an idyllic, unsuspecting summer sky. *This can't be happening.*

Things only got worse. I grew increasingly hopeless and depressed as I resisted the inevitability of being out.

I don't want to be gay. Don't know how to be gay. Too late to be gay now. Can't start life over at fifty. Can't rebuild on this ground.

As the year wore on, my despair grew deeper. In years past, when difficult times came my way, I turned to my faith in God. In more recent years, my self-loathing had generated a shroud that hid God from me and cut me off from any hope that I'd ever find spiritual life again.

I saw the sign for Reed College straight ahead at the intersection of SE 28th and Woodstock. I parked, sat for a moment and fingered the keys in my hand, put them back in the ignition, took them out again. I may have come out, albeit unwillingly, but I simply couldn't find the grace to come *in* to what it meant to be gay. With some energy I couldn't claim as my own, I left the car and meandered toward the Chapel where the concert was to take place. I was going to be late.

I entered an empty, echoing corridor and quickly made my way to the chapel at the opposite end of the hall, to the foot of the stairwell that led to the second floor. Not another soul in sight. As I reached the foot of the stairs, I looked up and saw the woman standing erect, dressed in a flowing white dress that reached the floor, with a mass of bright red hair falling down her back, hands folded, as if in prayer. I froze the way the fearful mortals of the Bible did in the presence of the angelic messengers of God.

I love you Lord…

She began to sing the familiar church chorus, her strong, rich notes ringing through the open chamber above me.

...and I lift my voice

I closed my eyes and tried to remember what it felt like to have the music of grace swirl around me.

...worship you, O my soul...

Her voice began to fade as she stepped out of the foyer above me and into the small chapel. I quickly climbed the stairs to follow the music and reached the open door of the chapel just as Cynthia sat down at her piano and began to accompany herself on the song. She asked the congregation to join her. I stood motionless and hesitant at the open doorway. The long, dark, wooden pews were filled with men and women, arms raised, eyes closed, singing their love song to God. I spotted an empty seat in the back pew, on the aisle and slipped quietly into place. I took a deep breath. I knew the song by heart, but I couldn't make my mouth move. So I listened. And watched. The music of the congregation was unlike any I'd ever heard. Strong, complex harmonies rose together to fill the rafters above. I could feel the sound vibrate through my body. Cynthia stopped playing the piano on the small stage at the front of the chapel. As the piano fell away, the song of the congregation seemed to crescendo and fill the room like a thick smoke. Like the holy smoke of God in the tabernacle of the Israelites from the Sunday school stories I had heard so many times. Behind Cynthia, a set of open windows welcomed the filtered rays of afternoon sun that cast an ethereal glow around her. I felt myself growing weak and lightheaded. Then, as if someone in the rafters had reached down to grab my hands, I felt my arms being pulled upward and a warm tingling around my lips as soft, mumbling words began to trickle out.

I love you Lord...

I whispered the melody and slowly closed my eyes.

And I lift my voice...

The music grew thicker around me and suddenly I felt

grace, mercy, forgiveness dancing close to me. Lightly kissing my cheeks. Brushing past my lips. Coaxing the slight tear from my eyes. Surrounding me with their strange tongues and their warm touch. Cynthia transposed into another song. A familiar call.

Softly and tenderly, Jesus is calling…

Without a break, the congregation followed her and their collective voices soared. Suddenly, but gently, a breeze began to blow through the open windows on one side of the chapel. Cool, summer wind flooded the holy place washing past me like a refreshing stream. Then, for a moment, the breeze became a rushing, mighty wind that rattled through the room and fell on me like a new Pentecost.

In the last days… I will pour out my Spirit on all flesh and your young men will see visions, and your old men will dream dreams.

The words of the scriptures filled my mind and for the first time I felt grace, mercy, and forgiveness embrace me like they might not let go. Here I was, singing my love song to God with a room full of queers, embraced by the God I thought was forever hidden behind a wall of shame and self-loathing. As the song reached its final verse, I fell back in the pew and released a long breath. It seemed some kind of energy had left my body. A demon exorcised. No guilt. No shame. Not for this moment. For the first time, I felt a sense of peace.

The piano started again and Cynthia moved into a different song. I opened my eyes and looked at the men and women around me. After almost fifty years, I knew I had crossed over to another shore. And here, in the fading July light of the chapel, I began to dream my dreams of other bridges and new shores I might now be free to walk.

The Trailer
Megan Kruse

L aurie and I bought the trailer for $500 from a man up in
Kelso. It was ten feet long, cracked and boxy, with torn
linoleum and mildew in the cabinets.

"She needs a little fixing up," he said, leading us to where it
was parked, eaten with rust spots, the paint peeling. When he
opened the door the handle fell off in his hand.

We were saying the things that you say when you're
grasping—maybe some couples say, *Let's have a baby,* or, *Let's
get a dog.* We said, *Let's get a dirty trailer and sell all of our things
and take it down to Mexico.* I hitched the trailer to my truck
and drove it fishtailing down the freeway. I parked it a block
off of Killingsworth, half on the shoulder. The aluminum sides
were hot in the August sun.

It began to look beautiful to me, almost hopeful, as it
leaned rakishly on the side of the street. When I had a cheap
vodka headache and Laurie was turned away from me in bed I
would think, *This is clearly the answer.*

I wanted badly to leave Portland.

In the 1968 Aristocrat Lo-Liner, far from this city, I was
sure that my girlfriend would begin to love me again, slowly at
first and then with great abandon. *I love you with abandon,* she

said in the careful dream I'd created, silhouetted against the line of the ocean. In the dream we played cards for hours at the tiny trailer table, and I had a set of plastic dishes that wouldn't break when we pitched over the rough Mexican roads.

That was what was supposed to happen.

Instead, I climbed from a bluish dream to Laurie's face wavering above the bed. *What do you want to do,* she said. *Because I can't do this anymore.* It wasn't a question. She carefully folded her clothes into three garbage bags and walked them the twenty blocks to her new girlfriend's house. Like that it was done.

I lay there for a few hours in the dust cold, the silhouettes of empty bottles lining the walls like a cityscape. We had sold all of our things for Mexico, moved into a basement apartment where the sounds were muted. *I feel crazy here,* I told Laurie, *I feel underwater.* She lit another bowl, turned up the television and said, *You* are *crazy.* It was one thing we could agree on. I had the distinct feeling that there were hundreds of things I could never say filling my body like a heavy, choking sand, an inventory of things I wanted or remembered: strong bourbon, to be held very tightly, the smell of my mother's perfume in the Dodge on the way to Port Angeles. And darker, mustier-smelling things, regrets and windblown promises.

At six in the evening I got up and made the bed. *A crazy person would not make the bed,* I thought. A crazy person would stay there all day, maybe all week. A crazy person might throw all of the blankets off onto the concrete floor and then decide to sleep on them, like a nest, but I was dressing, careful not to wear anything that belonged to Laurie, careful not to make any noise. It seemed important that there be quiet.

I locked the apartment and walked up Killingsworth. Late August, the sharp glare of discarded cans on the roadside, a crowd of teenage boys outside the market waiting for someone to buy them beer. A dull noise, the faded hum of summer. I turned up 15th toward Alberta, toward the bar where I was sure Bree would be. At night I could draw a map of where she'd be sitting, a path through the bright of bottles, crushed cigarettes.

She was right where I expected her, at the back of the bar, leaning over a notebook. Once I thought I might be in love with her, but in the wistful way that you love someone when you know from the beginning that it will never really be returned, and if it is then you won't want it anymore.

"You look like shit," Bree said.

"Laurie left," I said. "She's gone."

Bree and I had spoken less and less in the last few weeks—silence lapped over me as things got worse with Laurie, and I knew Bree could see it. The last time I saw her I told her a little about Mexico, smiling hard. She pushed the hair out of my eyes; I had to go to the bathroom and smoke three cigarettes over the dented toilet before I could stand to go back and look at her again.

We drank Bushmills from the bar and from the bottle she kept in her bag and she told me that it would be all right, that it was better. All the things you say. She had a new girlfriend, Anna. A girl I remembered vaguely, with narrow hips, stringy blonde hair; a loose, easy beauty. She was drinking Bushmills and talking about Anna while I concentrated hard on chewing my nails. Bree was Tennessee-ragged; I had watched her drink a fifth of Jack at ten o'clock in the morning and still shoot a straight line of tin cans off the edge of the porch. I lit a cigarette. She always had a new girlfriend. When she tired of one she stopped calling. *There's nothing to talk about,* she'd say. *But listen, I just met this new girl.* It was part of what she didn't understand—why I would stay with Laurie while every bar in the city had a circle of dykes haloed in cigarette smoke and spilled drinks that I could push myself toward. I wasn't sure I understood myself. Only that it was easier to watch the thing between us grow more and more ruined than to let it go and know I'd failed.

"Bree," I said, "I don't know what to do." My throat felt thick. I wanted her to tell me where to go next, to tell me again that it would be all right. That I wasn't all the things Laurie said. We stood at the bar. My eyes stung.

Bree was swaying, her cigarette a long gray ash. She wrapped her arms around my neck. I could smell the bourbon on her. The room felt light, shifting; her tongue was quick and wet in my mouth.

Then we were in the dark of her car, the painted lines weaving across the road. The passenger-seat window was cold against my cheek. The stairs, her apartment, the top floor of her creaking house. For a second I felt it again, the feeling I'd had when I first met her, at some terrible house party, both of us drunk on gas station champagne. And then our clothes were off; I pushed against her hard. For a second she was Laurie, and everything was all right again. The room seemed to spin and she was still Laurie, but the real Laurie, the one who said, in her slow, Midwestern drawl, *You're lucky to have me—some people wouldn't put up with your bullshit.* My face was too warm. I opened my eyes and it was Bree, pulling me on top of her, her hands moving quick, cheek against my chest. For a second desire was a thick pulling rope and then the feeling was gone, replaced by a dull fear. I wanted to be at home, alone in the underwater basement, not in the dark with my best friend. *What are we doing,* I thought. I had forgotten how things could slip, how inexact it all was.

In the morning we adjusted our clothes, avoided each other's eyes. *There's nothing to talk about.* As I was leaving I looked out her windows. It seemed that overnight the trees had all burst out in yellow fall, and none of the scenery was familiar anymore.

Laurie came back to get the rest of her things. She looked quickly from me to the door. "We just need time," she said. "And then I'm sure we can be friends." Her neck was bruised with someone else's teeth. She'd dyed her long hair darker. It was in her eyes and when she smiled it wasn't a smile I'd seen before.

We'd moved in together in a rush of good intentions and need—she left her boyfriend and I lost a roommate. We were acquaintances when we both lived in Ohio. When we collided again in Portland, we were more. The house filled with our small holdings; there was lichen on the windows, not enough money—I brought home rolls of stamps, a rake, powdered milk that transformed beneath the faucet, watched the way the river seemed to burn at dusk and felt full and rich with ordinary enchantments. *The good thing about us,* Laurie liked to say, *is that we were friends first. So if this ends, it'll all be fine.*

"You should probably look for a job," she said. "You always feel better when you're working." I had quit my restaurant job two weeks earlier, presumably because we were going to be lying in the sand somewhere near Cabo. Laurie called an automated system each week, punched in the numbers to say she had been looking for work, collected an unemployment check. I *had* liked the restaurant, but mostly because it kept me away from the house, from Laurie's dependable sting. The bright of glasses, silverware flats clouded in steam; the faces of strangers swam through a comforting heat.

"You do," she said. "You used to say so yourself. Why don't you just go ask them to give you your job back?" I just looked at her. Her arms were crossed. I tried to remember the last time she had touched me. "You don't have to look like that," she snapped. She went to the bookshelf, heaving a stack of her old textbooks into her arms. "These are mine."

"That's my dictionary," I said, pointing to the book on the bottom of the pile. I'd taken it from my mother's house when I moved out.

"No," Laurie said. "It's not. I bought it for school."

There were gray holes in my memory, I thought, like time was an accelerating car and the scenery was starting to blur, small towns with no landmarks between them. Still, I remembered its broken red spine and the way the letters had looked like code, ancient things under my tracing finger, the pages thin, the smell of smoke and age. Laurie dropped the dictionary and it fell with a hard sound. *G. Greeting, grenade, grenadier.*

"Take it," she said. "If it's that important to you." She went back into the bedroom and came back with the pillows. "I bought these," she said. "Your old one is in the closet."

When she left I picked up the dictionary. "It *is* important," I said aloud. I had the feeling of tin foil held between my teeth.

The damp basement, stacked bottles; I learned how to not be alone in Portland, how to stop up the day with small talk and strangers. I had been in the city for four years. Bree and I spent the first two stealing kale and tomatoes from the public garden left unlocked, bread from behind the 42nd Street bakery, leaning out of Bree's window to smoke cigarettes and watch the street sink slow into the evening.

And then her mother died. A blood clot—she collapsed in a movie theater and it was that detail that Bree kept coming back to—stale popcorn, soda on the carpet. Bree lost twenty pounds. One afternoon we lay in her twin bed and her knees bruised up against me. *I feel like I can hardly breathe,* she said, *I don't feel like myself.*

I was sure my arms could wrap around her twice.

I'm so cold, she said.

I wanted badly to give her something, felt sure that if I could only figure out what it was then it would all be undone, the death, the cold. Instead I put her in my sweater and we drove an hour east to the mineral baths in Carson. We sat in the dim light, in the sulfur smell and wet curtains, until she said she felt warm again.

Slowly, things got better, until one day were downtown and Bree surveyed the band in the Courthouse Square, took a long drink from her coffee cup of whiskey, and shouted, *Won't somebody play some goddamn Johnny Cash around here?* You've come back, I thought.

Now the phone was silent on the wall. Without Bree the day stretched like a long panic. *Tell me what we'll be like when we're old,* she liked to say. *When we're two old lesbos with brittle bones and cat hair on our pants.*

But then I remembered her narrowed eyes, a month or two before, when some girl she'd slept with had kept calling. *I mean, really—Doesn't she get it?*

I walked to her bar, half-hoping she would be there, half-hoping she wouldn't. The table at the back was empty. I sat at the bar instead and the bartender told me stories about her African parrot, how it could make a noise like a typewriter cartridge and say, *Leave already, I want to jerk off,* when guests stood up from the table.

"Where's your friend?" the bartender asked. I shrugged. She had nine or ten silver bracelets sliding up and down her wrists. She took them off when it got busy. When she went into the back for more glasses I took one, slipped it into my pocket.

"Do you want to stay until I get off?" she asked. "We could go out by the airport, sit by the river." I imagined us fucking in the cold sand, the planes low over the water. In my pocket her bracelet was cool against my fingertips.

"I can't," I said. The conversations around me led nowhere, paused, faded away.

The tiny screened windows, doll's oven; I left the bar and sat in the trailer in the dark. I felt tired. I folded the table down so it was flat and lay back on it, staring at the wedge of faint stars out the window.

Outside someone was shuffling through the recycling. My eyes felt heavy; the sound of breaking glass, then things that moved in and out of the dark: a silver ring, a raincoat. Photographs of strangers. Sage dried for burning. A bass drum. Tin prayer cards for a baby, a hurt leg, a bruised heart. *If your house was burning, what would you save?* A voice that sounded like my own. Lists of things I wanted; lists of things I'd lost. If I could only hold onto everything, I thought, then I would know exactly who to be. The wind was the gas left on, a slow poison rubbing its back against the mattress. *I can't breathe*, I thought, but when I opened my eyes it was light again. I knew I must have slept.

The rusted penknife on the counter; pushpins in the siding; the freezer thrown open; it must be well into the morning, I thought. A fly buzzed from the corner and an earwig skittered into the mouth of the sink, eye like a pin. I knew suddenly: I should just go.

The air outside felt clean and cool and I walked to buy a coffee. It was simple, I thought. I couldn't think of why I hadn't thought of it before. I didn't need Laurie in order to leave. If I was in the trailer, heading toward some quiet beach, then all of these things would be stripped of their petty worth.

Even the tragedies would be small ones: *Where has the map gone? I need more gasoline.*

Two days later, Laurie called. Her voice seemed to be coming from far away. "I heard you've been sleeping with all of Northeast," she said. I heard her clear her throat.

"I'm leaving," I said. "In the trailer."

Someone in the background whispered something. "You won't make it in that trailer," she said. "It's not safe. You'll break down before you get to Salem."

Bree was good at these things—she would say, *Don't call her. Call me if you feel like you're going to call her. Like a sponsor.*

"You need to buy me out of the trailer," she said.

Bree would say, *I don't like the way that she talks to you.*

"I don't think this is any of your business," I said finally. A thrill like electrical current, bee sting; I thought of my grandmother, steel-faced, saying, *Every pretty girl is a warning.* "Don't call me anymore." I hung up the phone and laughed. The smallest fortune, relief like a coin in my hand. I remembered being seventeen, when spring became summer and then the gray fall. I was busy with my first girlfriend, smoking cigarettes down by the Sound, tending to this new secret that was love, that I was sure I'd invented. I wanted that feeling again. I wanted Laurie gone for good. I started to dial Bree's number, then put the receiver back down. It wasn't time. If I left, I knew, things would be better. I imagined sitting at the trailer table, writing her a letter, saying, *I'm filling this envelope with Mexican sand, think of me, I miss you.* And then, weeks or months later, when I drove the trailer—it would be worse for the wear, I thought, but still upright, still hopeful—back into the city, things would be back to normal, and we could all get on with it.

That afternoon I went out to work on the trailer. I would paint the inside white, I thought. A bright white that drew the sun. When I was alone everything would be cleaner, as though I'd begun again.

I squinted down the sidewalk. There was an empty space where the trailer had been.

I walked up and down the street, as though maybe someone would pull up with the rusting box of it bumping behind them, saying, *Sorry, I thought this was mine. Just returning it to its illegal parking spot.* For a second I thought about going to Laurie, to tell her, but turned and walked back home instead. It was an old habit, I thought. The hope that if you put yourself close enough to someone you will know them, that every empty corner will fill with all the things that are passing between you. The space on the street dragged like a thin wire through me, a sweet, piercing sorrow.

When I was young I kept a drawer in a bureau filled with salt and pepper shakers, scarves, ceramic figurines—a tiny, useless inheritance secreted away in the guest room. I would take them out one by one, hold them, return them to the drawer. As though they could conspire to give me meaning, a small religion, something important built of smaller things. A church that was as powerful as my ability to memorize, to keep. And now, I thought, things were running like water, right through my hands.

I knocked on Bree's door. She looked tired when she opened the screen.

"It's gone," I said.

She glanced behind her and I could see a girl inside, lying upside down on the sofa with her bare feet on the wall. Anna, I thought. Her new girlfriend. I wondered if she knew that I had been in Bree's bed.

"It's gone," I said again. "The trailer."

She looked at me. Behind her Anna's pale feet drummed against the wall, her hair a wash of blonde brushing against the floor. Bree was studying my face and then I was crying. I sat down on the step. She put her hand on my arm and pulled me up.

"Let's go," she said. "Come on." She pulled her jacket from the back of a chair and kissed Anna. We walked out to her Jeep. There was a chill in the air. It was terrible to be in Portland in the winter, when no one went outside. Mexico seemed very far away.

It was starting to rain as we got onto the highway. The baths were in an old hotel, gray and strange as an asylum, set back in the woods an hour east of Portland. The rain was hard by the time Bree stopped the car. I thought of her hand moving inside of me, how it felt both strange and familiar, how later I wished we hadn't.

We undressed, slowly, in a narrow room with two stools and a long mirror. A woman in a white dress led us to twin bathtubs and poured the water. "You soak here for thirty minutes, and then we wrap you," she said. Her voice was gravel rolling in a tin can. It was too hot. I moved up under the tap, poured cold water over my wrists.

We sat there for a long time, not speaking, before the woman in the white dress came back. "Are you ready to get out?" she asked.

I felt like a child.

We followed her to the next room. Twelve flat cots, white sheets stiff as paper.

Bree lay down. The woman wrapped her in the gray wool blankets, tightly.

When she came to me I looked away.

Rain, heat, water pouring into a porcelain tub in the next

room; *I can lose the pillows,* I thought. *And the dictionary.* I would move out of the basement, start again at the restaurant. Tonight Anna would unzip her dress, step out of it cleanly, pull Bree's arms around her. A dozen blocks away Laurie would turn, turn again, and finally sleep. The simplicity of this, the predictability, felt important. I would not get the trailer back.

I once read about a museum display, an exhibit of things that have been recovered from bodies. The reporter spoke to visitors, pale voices in print, *I wanted to learn about need. I wanted to be full. I came to see what I had survived.* Scalpel, dildo, IUD, tampon; *I wanted returned what was taken from me;* bullets. Stitches, bobby pins. Smoke, folded into a sterile cloth. Your stupid mouth, I thought, your breasts, your heart, your hands.

When we left the sky was darkening. Bree had a pint of whiskey wedged under the seat of the car. We passed it back and forth as she drove, faster and faster through the Gorge. "I'm sorry about what happened," she said suddenly. "Between us, I mean."

"I know," I said. "Me too."

Back in the city, Bree drove us out to the bluffs and let the car idle. She pulled me toward her and kissed my cheek. I leaned against her. I remembered how the hair had curled damp on her forehead when I'd driven her home from the baths two years ago, the highway splitting through walls of rock, the wet-dark city ahead of us. I loaned her a dress for her mother's funeral. It hung off of her and later she left it in Memphis, threw it over the back of a sofa after the service. She looked terrible in that dress.

Bree turned the heat all the way up and wound the windows down. The whiskey was hot on the back of my throat. She reached over, squeezed my hand. We sat there for a long time and she didn't let go. I looked out toward the river.

"I want everything to be OK again," Bree said. "I miss you."

There are a hundred ways we try to rescue each other, I thought, and it didn't seem so big anymore.

Down below us the lit warehouses were a bowl of tiny lights. "I miss you, too," I said. Just out of sight the bridges were stringing through the air; her hand; this certain warmth. There were never any sirens, I thought. No real way to tell where you were meant to be. Just the slow rain, and outside the road stretching empty; then sometimes this feeling of home.

Gay Apparel
Lois Leveen

I adore all my friends who are friends of Dorothy, but please don't call me a fag hag.

I see myself more as a kicky, kikey, camp vamp. Just the latest in a line of sexy, funny, loud-mouthed Jewish dames who share an innate affinity with arch gay men. It's a generously-bosomed genealogy that includes Bette Midler and Barbra Streisand. Not to mention Liz Taylor, if you count converts, and Mae West, if you count anyone whose mother was Jewish, which, following a distinguished rabbinical tradition, I do.

As that Dorothy of all Dorothies (and don't be fooled by the Parker, which was her married name—she was also a member of my tribe) might have put it:

Please don't call me a hag,
that sounds awful shrewish.
I just adore every fag
'cause I'm a boysterous Jewess.

Maybe it's no coincidence that I've spent my adult life in the great queer meccas of North America—San Francisco, Vancouver BC, West Hollywood. Portland, however, is a different kind of queer, a veritable modern day land of Lesbos. Which is great if you want to comparison-shop Subarus or play a few innings of womyn's softball. But if you want to dress up, nibble fabulous hors d'oeuvres, and engage in witty repartee—and I do—you have to go where the boys are.

This is why there could be no better place for me to spend the fifth night of Hanukkah than up in Arlington Heights at Robert and Will's Christmas party.

I met Robert and Will at a Halloween party. I was wearing the scariest costume there, actually a group costume I roped my partner Chuck and our friend David (of course David is gay, why are you even wondering?) into wearing too. We went as Cathy with a C, Kathy with a K, and Cathi with an i—the girls from HR. Wearing blond wigs and the ugliest Christmas sweaters we could find at Goodwill, we spent the evening offering up trays of Christmas cookies and shrieking, "Don't you just love the office holiday party?" and "Here comes the UPS guy, where's the damn mistletoe?"

But Robert and Will's soiree is no time for Christmas sweaters, not when I've got dozens of fabulous frocks waiting to come out of the closet. Chuck has spent enough time around me and my 'mos that he qualifies for near-queer—sort of the O'Douls of hetero dates. Not only can I dress him up as Cathy for Halloween, I can count on him for help making the crucial but subtle choice between the vintage sixties cocktail dress with the sequins accenting the cleavage, or the vintage sixties cocktail dress with the rhinestones accenting the cleavage. He even knows exactly what to tell me as I'm about to leave the house in tonight's winner, a sleek little sleeveless number, when it's thirty-eight Oregon degrees outside: "Don't forget your elbow gloves."

Elbow gloves have a certain faggish gravitational force, and moments after we arrive at Robert and Will's, really just as soon I've planted some big red-lipstick kisses on our hosts, Chuck and I find ourselves in Gay Central Station.

"Look at all this meat," Chuck says.

I'm relieved to realize he's referring to the antipasto. Twenty-Four Hour Fitness may just as well have cut back to Eighteen-and-a-Half tonight, because every gym bunny in Portland is hopping around here. When someone introduces me to "Brian with the dimples," I can't help but inquire whether the reference is to his facial features or to some other anatomical area entirely.

Chuck is quickly lured off by two nice young men who offer him a blow-pop. Perhaps I should be concerned that he's taking candy from strangers, but I'm too busy being surrounded by so much fabulousness. I am truly in my element. That element being crushed velvet jackets and muscle tees. The boys and I are trading quips like characters in a Truman Capote story when I overhear another guest say, "I heard Lois is here."

I turn to discover the speaker is some woman I've never met. For a moment I think this means I have truly joined the ranks of Bette and Barbra, and now have bona fide fans. Will crushes this dream like it was so much ice in his banana daiquiri, explaining that there's another Lois in attendance, someone he knows from work. The from-work contingent are easy to spot—the only straight people here, near-queer Chuck and I excepted. I immediately go in search of the other Lois.

She's hanging out next to the bar. I like her already. We quickly confirm all we have in common: a name, a sign (Scorpio), and a ribald sense of humor. Noticing my purple glasses and purple suede pumps, she says knowingly, "that's my favorite color."

Alas, I cannot live a lie. I confess that my fave color is actually faux leopard, though I declare diplomatically that purple is an excellent accent color. This Lois Common Denominator settles it. For the rest of the evening, we serve as a Lois-Lois bridge across the hetero/homo divide, ensuring that the crowd from IBM has a user-friendly interface with the crowd of G-A-Y.

When Chuck finds me sometime around midnight and asks if I'm having fun, the answer is obvious from the quintessence of queers surrounding me. There's Andrew, whom I met at a New Year's Eve party a couple of years ago—I was in elbow gloves, he was enthralled. Robert and Will, whom I met at Andrew's Halloween party. Marc and Floyd, whom I met at a pre-Passover casserole potluck, the last bit of leavening before eight days wandering the Manischewitz desert. And a whole new bevy of boys I've met here tonight. Even if I don't see them again until Robert and Will's next Christmas party, we'll kiss and coo then like we're the oldest, dearest friends in the world.

Because, queer Portland, divas like us are drawn together by that one divine truth: there's no place like homo for the holidays.

Field Day
Lynn Barkley

Yesterday was field day at Matt's school. I was worried, and determined to experience every moment of it with him. So I signed up to volunteer—all day long.

I was assigned to work the "Junkyard Relay Race" station, which was next to the "Burlap Sack Relay Race" where Matt's class began the day. Our station was quiet, so I had a front row seat for Matt's opening event. It was a typical Portland June morning, overcast and a little cool but—unfortunately—no chance of a rain out.

Matt's fourth grade teacher blew the whistle and the first student in each line hopped off in earnest. It was starting out a very close race. My heart pounded harder. Soon it would be Matt's turn to climb into the burlap sack, jump forty yards down the field, turn, step out of the sack, race back to the start line, and hand off the sack to the next child. I kept hoping, wishing, willing that before Matt's turn something would happen to break the succession of talented children effortlessly climbing into their bags, leaping down the field, deftly turning, stepping out of the burlap, and speeding back to the lines. Certainly one of these children would tangle or trip. Certainly someone would break the perfect rhythm.

Matt has Asperger's Syndrome, an autism spectrum condition. And one of the many ways it manifests is in his sensory functioning. As his occupational therapist explained to me and his other mom, he's confused about where his body is in space. To most people, he just seems incredibly clumsy.

But my ill hopes for the other fourth graders were denied. Matt's turn arrived without mishap. Predictably, he struggled to get into the bag. He fell twice as he jumped slowly and deliberately down the field.

Another kid on his team screamed at Matt: "Go! Hurry-up!"

Matt stopped short of the turn-around pylon and was motionless for several seconds, probably allowing his mind to process the next few movements of turning and climbing out of the bag. He tangled in the bag as he tried to get out.

Over and over the other kid screeched, "GO, HURRY-UP, GO, HURRY-UP, GO, HURRY-UP."

Matt fell over one more time and his shoe came off in the bag. By the time he fished his shoe from the bag, slipped it on, and headed back to his line, he'd been lapped twice by the other teams.

The "hurry up!" kid flailed his arms and stomped his feet in frustration.

I was furious at that kid. I wanted to run over and stuff one of the burlap sacks into his mouth. I wanted to scream at him to shut up, that Matt was trying his best, that it was hard for him. But I just stood there and realized that, years ago, I was that kid yelling hurry-up. I was the one on the playground who screamed at the fat kid or the awkward kid or the confused kid. At my fourth-grade birthday party, my mom had to pull me aside and explain that it was hurtful to choose kick ball teams by having each of the captains pick one "good" kid and one "bad" kid. My whole life revolved around the world of winners and losers, better than and worse than, not as good as. As I grew up, I obsessed over failures and paid little attention to successes. I rode my bike across the country, averaging one hundred miles a day, but I focused on the time I was soundly defeated in my first cycling race. I never entered another cycling competition. Opportunities passed me by. I refused to take chances for fear of failure. It all made my world smaller. But maybe all that was my problem, not Matt's.

As the morning progressed, I kept looking around to see how Matt was doing. Every time I'd catch a glimpse of him, he was clapping, jumping up and down, smiling.

When we met up at lunch I asked him if he'd had fun.

He beamed. "It was awesome."

Stage Zero
Jacqueline Raphael

I move to Portland to transcend my East Coast upbringing: To work less, worry less, and though I cringe to admit it, love myself more. Still, I can't help rolling my eyes when the tattooed girl on a bicycle on Alberta Street says Portland is a place for healing.

"You bet, darling," my girlfriend, Leanne, says. She taps my arm. "You against healing or something?"

"Sorry," I mumble. "I'm not good at New Age."

Leanne sighs. A native Oregonian, she doesn't always find my New York sarcasm appealing. I am practicing gratitude, however, since Portland has changed my life. Now I have a forty-hour-a-week job I like, a beautiful girlfriend with a positive attitude, a new condo needing almost no maintenance. I even have a counselor I can talk to for a mere $10 co-pay thanks to my company's health insurance plan.

"I have a couple little things to deal with," I tell Jessica, the counselor, in our first session. In the big scheme of things, my issues are minor: some relationship difficulties, a lackluster career. "Quickly," I add. "I don't want to spend a lot of time on this."

"I'm not a magician," Jessica says. "People change when

they're ready. But maybe, if you're lucky, something will happen to speed it along."

Something does. In March, I get a call at my office from Providence Portland. The nurse says I need to have my mammogram redone. A few days later I'm in a lab and a radiologist, Dr. Blackman, hits a switch. My friend Barbara and I see three pairs of breasts outlined in white against a black background. My breasts in triplicate. It's as if we're looking out from the deck of the *Starship Enterprise* at the galaxy looming ahead. Dr. Blackman points to the center of my right breast. I squint; he motions me closer. He points until finally I see an indistinct cluster of tiny white spots, like rock salt sprinkled onto dark rye bread.

"Calcifications. Probably normal," he says, switching on the lights. He wheels himself over to his desk and studies my file. "I'm almost certain it's nothing. But you're only forty-one. Just as a precaution, let's be sure."

"So tell me again why you're seeing a counselor," my girlfriend asks, lying in my arms. She has asked me before. I'm beginning to think she has a counselor who's advised her to ferret out the dirt about me before getting any closer.

"I want as much self-awareness as possible," I say, gesturing at the fields of self-awareness just beyond us.

She smirks, then tilts her head to study me. "Don't you have enough self-awareness already?" she asks.

"You can never have enough self-awareness," I say. But my response is still a lie. After several months, I still can't admit I'm not yet over my parents' rage and selfishness and the consequences of their divorce so many years ago. The puny little problems of my childhood growing inside me like a cancer.

It's not the East Coast inside me that needs to be slayed, Jessica has suggested. It's something else.

"I'm not happy about the scar," I say to Dr. Lane, a breast surgeon. For the second time he explains that he must perform a surgical rather than a needle biopsy. He assures me he'll do his best, but there will be a two-inch scar perpendicular to the edge of my aureole, like a tiny T-square.

"It's ridiculous, all this fuss for nothing," my mother says on the telephone, "and then you'll be stuck with a scar."

"I've never been with anyone who gets so much pleasure from her breasts," Leanne says one morning. It surprised me the first time, too. One day my breasts were stroked for so long that the hot, ticklish feeling turned over inside me and I screamed. I couldn't even believe I was coming. I begged my lover to do it again. The next time, my breasts were primed and it didn't take as long. Soon it was easy. "Is it just heavenly to be so into sex all the time?" Leanne asks.

This isn't the first time a woman has commented on how much I emphasize sex. Planning it, having it, talking about it afterward. The women aren't complaining. Like Leanne, they're just curious about what it means to me. I tell her as much as I can about the inchoate feelings that become so intense. There's always something I'm after: an ease in my body and my mind, the confidence combined with effort and stamina.

It took over a year in college to admit my feelings for women. But ever since, my erogenous zones have led me to my truths. My clitoris once decided to play dead throughout a relationship, refusing to be aroused by anything that didn't resemble a power tool. I worried, then finally broke down and bought the power tool. It didn't save the relationship, but it saved me.

There were many other lessons. I learned about my body slowly. I learned my body knows me better than I know myself. I learned to love it well.

"I just wish I knew you better," Leanne says suddenly, looking a little sad.

"What do you mean?" My voice rises. Why is it that talking about sex almost never brings two women closer? Is it impossible to describe to another woman what you feel inside your body? Is it over when you need to try? "This is a way to know me better," I say. Leanne gives me a side hug and apologizes.

After the biopsy, I'm stuck with more than a scar. But like my other problems, the bad cells growing in my right breast aren't very bad. I have what Dr. Lane calls "early cancer." On a pad of paper he draws the plumbing of the breast—all ducts and lobules—and several diagrams depicting stages of unhealthy cell growth. My bad cells aren't wandering outside my duct or forming a mass. I don't have invasive cancer and my life's not in danger.

"You have what's called DCIS. Stage zero," Dr. Lane concludes.

"Zero?" I repeat. "Isn't that, like, nothing?" I smile but he doesn't.

"No," he says slowly, "but it's the best cancer diagnosis you could have."

The only problem with DCIS, I learn, is that it *may* turn into invasive cancer, and no one knows which DCIS will and which won't. It also puts me at high risk for invasive breast cancer in the future. Dr. Lane explains that he will remove the remaining DCIS. Then I will undergo radiation and take tamoxifen to fight future cancer. Tamoxifen will chemically alter my body, plunging me into premature menopause. Hot flashes, vaginal dryness, and other unsexy developments.

"Are you kidding?" I cry. "Just because I *might* get "real" cancer later?"

"It's standard procedure," says Dr. Lane, glancing at the clock on the wall, "to keep you from getting cancer again."

"Menopause comes eventually," says Barbara, trying to be positive.

First a scar, now this?

Dr. Lane leans in. "At least it's not a mastectomy," he says. It feels like he's punched me in the stomach, but maybe I had it coming. Maybe you don't complain when you have stage zero cancer. Dr. Lane rises, tears the papers from his pad and hands them to me. "Mary will schedule your surgery and give you the name of a radiation oncologist. Have a good day."

"He had no right to scare you that way, talking about a mastectomy," my mother says on the telephone. "And for God's sake, get a second opinion about that drug. Your grandmother had a horrific time during menopause—thank God I had the hysterectomy—and I don't want you starting that any earlier than you need to. Plus, I hate to say it but menopause ages you terribly." She pauses.

I try to relax but it's useless.

"Don't they have better doctors than that in Portland?" she adds.

I'll get a new doctor, I decide. I drive home full of gratitude for my health insurance.

Three days and a slew of calls and emails later, I'm at St. Vincent's, a hospital set against a backdrop of rolling green hills. My new female breast surgeon, Dr. Jones, sails into my exam room wearing a royal blue dress under her lab coat. She is tall and gorgeous. She looks into my eyes and smiles. "I'm going to take care of you," she says. I feel doubtful, relieved.

Dr. Jones feels like the real thing. If I have to cope with breast cancer in the sticks, I at least want the best doctor in town. Hundreds of women, including former Portland Mayor Vera Katz, have trusted Dr. Jones with their breasts. An MRI is scheduled, just as a precaution. Dr. Jones also says I should take tamoxifen for five years. I frown and she puts her hand on my arm. "Don't worry about that now. Take things one day at a time, and you'll be fine." She hugs me at the end of our appointment.

Being taken care of can make me feel like a child. But this time, I try to be the child I never was, the one who doesn't worry, who says "OK" and trusts the adults in her life.

During the breast MRI I lie face down with my breast hanging in a sling beneath me. I'm rolled under the dome of the MRI magnet, and must remain still, especially when the machine beeps and bangs and clicks, when the magnetic resonance images of my breast are being produced. Finally, I'm pulled out of the tunnel. Weak from so much effort at keeping still, I limp back to my cubicle and slip on my clothes. An hour later I'm upstairs in Dr. Jones' office talking to her assistant about my formerly good left breast. Apparently, the MRI shows eight highly suspicious areas.

"That's in your left breast," she reminds me. "We don't know about your right yet."

"What are you saying?" I ask.

"It's nearly impossible they're all cancer," the assistant continues, "and MRIs can give false positives." Good, I'm thinking. Keep talking that way. "But these spots look just like your early cancer. Obviously we can't biopsy them all, so we'll probably start by biopsying the largest spot on the left. Hopefully, it will be nothing. But if it's DCIS, or worse, then Dr. Jones will want to have a talk with you."

I don't call my mother in the parking lot this time. I don't call anyone for a while. When I do call Leanne, I don't sound tough at all.

"You don't have to explain," Leanne whispers into the phone. "Just come over." But when I fall into her open arms, I keep talking. It's strange. I can't stop. I keep repeating what the nurse said. All those spots can't be cancer, not the scary kind, anyway. But just one of them might be. The tears just fall, as if someone else is crying them.

Three days later I'm back at St. Vincent's for an MRI-guided biopsy. Because MRIs can be misleading, the radiologist tells me it's possible he won't see any irregularities and we won't need to do a biopsy. Once again I lay face down on the examination table, strapped in to prevent movement that would blur the images. Once again my breast is placed into a cushioned compartment. When the clicking and pulsing start, I lie more still than last time, to achieve a clear image so I can go home. After fifteen minutes the nurse says we're done and I'm pulled out of the dome. She unstraps me but says not to move.

"You OK?" she asks.

I nod, still lying face down. I am eager to hear good news. The radiologist appears.

"Are you ready for the biopsy?" he asks, and once again the tears come pouring out.

The nurse notices and puts her hand on my shoulder. "Honey, it's OK. It won't hurt."

"Let's get started," the radiologist says, bringing his stool up beside me. He angles the machine with the needle underneath my breast, and the nurse hands him his gloves and tools as I silently continue weeping.

"I don't want to talk about my girlfriend, or sex, or even my breasts today," I say to Jessica, sitting on her tan couch, staring at the walls I've studied for almost six months.

"OK. Something else you'd prefer to discuss?"

"Yeah. It' something—no, it's lots of things that happened when I was eleven, twelve, thirteen. Not horrible things…" I trail off and Jessica frowns. "Important things," I add.

"Like what?"

"Like feeling alone." I cringe. What happened to the no-nonsense Jersey girl I used to be? Will I ever stop with all this neurotic shit about myself? Still, Jessica says healing doesn't happen until you accept *all* of your loss—the pain and grief and scars. "Like knowing my parents abandoned me," I continue. "Not literally, but getting so caught up in themselves after the divorce. So pissed off and self-centered. Their dating dramas. All those years I needed to talk to them."

"What would you say?"

"You guys…sucked." It sounds ridiculous.

She laughs. "That's a great start," she says, nodding as I talk faster about my parents.

Am I really still upset by how my father screamed and my mother turned and left my brother and me standing in the marble foyer, overnight bags in hand, unable to decide whether to walk out the door? No matter what I say Jessica nods. I glance at my watch and wonder how we'll get to the end of this story. Turns out we need to continue this in the next session, and the next.

To my surprise, I don't say I want to crush my parents between steel plates or slash them with knives. I don't shit my pants. I don't even want to kill myself for being an unlovable and cruel child. "I wanted my parents to love me more when they divorced, not less," I say, and the world doesn't collapse.

Leanne accompanies me to my next appointment with Dr.

Jones. My biopsy results: more DCIS, and much more of another kind of irregular cell growth not considered early cancer, but pre-cancer.

In the examination room we don't speak. Leanne leans over and hugs my arm. Dr. Jones comes in dressed in a paisley yellow blouse under her lab coat.

"Someone new," she says, turning to shake Leanne's hand. "Nice to meet you." Then she turns to me. No time for socializing.

"Your results weren't what we'd expected, as you know. So, we've got extensive pre-cancerous cell growth, bilateral early cancer, your age, some family history. Given what I've seen in my practice, I feel the best thing for you to do is to get a double mastectomy."

I wait for more but hear only silence.

"I only have two tiny spots of early cancer right now, and we don't really know what will happen with those," I say. Like, this is one side of the story, right? Dr. Jones smiles again, but I see darkness beneath the bright eyes shining up at me.

"Fifteen years ago, when I started out, I would have agreed with you. But I've seen hundreds of patients since then. Some never had a recurrence; others come back with cancer a couple years later. You look like someone who will be back soon. I wish I could say something different, but I don't think it's wise for you to wait."

"So you're saying Jacqueline's case is not typical?" Leanne asks.

Dr. Jones nods.

"I'd like to ask the questions first, please," I say in a voice I don't recognize. "This is all based on speculation, right?"

"No, it's my professional opinion."

"To be extra safe."

"To keep you alive," she says. "I believe you'll have more

problems in less time than you think. Five years, maybe ten. Maybe just one or two."

"But right now, not one of the irregular cells in my breasts is an invasive cancer."

Dr. Jones pauses. "Not yet," she says carefully. "As your doctor, I'll do whatever you want and I will treat you as well as I can. But this is my recommendation."

After the appointment, as Leanne and I cross the parking lot, I point out that Dr. Jones obviously stated her case as strongly as possible. "She just doesn't want me to take any chances. But of course it's not her decision."

Leanne stops walking. "Do you actually think this was about trying to persuade you? She said several times that your life may hang in the balance." Leanne sighs, then stares at the asphalt. "You don't mean you're actually considering not doing it, do you?"

"Of course I'm not going to just do it," I cry.

"You didn't hear a thing she said, did you?"

I can't respond. I'm not angry, just shocked. The conversation with Dr. Jones moved far beyond the line I'd drawn in my mind, the one I was willing to cross. I expected to hear a double mastectomy was a reasonable consideration, not the choice I should make.

Just like breasts, I see the doctors in pairs. Two breast surgeons, two radiation oncologists, two medical oncologists. I receive second, third, even fourth opinions. I tell each I want to discuss my options. Male or female, young or old, the doctors nod and sit forward in their chairs. After reviewing my file and listening to my history, they provide their recommendations.

With all of them, there is an eerie moment toward the end of the appointment. The doctor stands, shakes my hand, and wishes me luck with my decision. I am reluctant to end the appointment. I learn a medical opinion, even six medical opinions, isn't an answer. The doctor turns and walks out the door. I slip away wrapped in a fog. For hours I can be lost. Driving home, I don't see the Banfield winding in front of me. I don't talk on the phone any more. I review what I've heard, comparing it to what I've learned before.

At home I sometimes call my brother in New York City. At thirty five, he's survived colon cancer. We joke about our bad genes and laugh, giddy about how we're getting back at our cancer-free parents. We say how weird it would be if I let some crazy Portland doctor remove two of my erogenous zones.

I call Dr. Jones almost every week with a new question, and though it usually takes a few days, she always returns my call. More important, every time I leave a message, I feel a little less afraid of what's happening, a little less disconnected. I called. I did something. Now I am waiting for Dr. Jones to return my call. Everything is as good as it can be, and it is Dr. Jones' turn to call.

I've postponed seeing the plastic surgeons. The one with straight blonde hair laughs when I say I can't wait to look through his photo album. It's filled with bust shots, literally, meaning photos of breasts without heads. The second surgeon sits beside me at his computer showing me images, as if we're shopping online. For the plastic surgeons I have a special question: if I do this, will I have any sensation in my breasts? They say yes, I'll eventually have sensation in the breasts, but no sexual feeling in the nipples or aureoles. Their tone is professional when I ask again. Never, they say. They do not look away or say they're sorry. Tears flow easily now. It feels like some part of me, deep inside, is starting to understand something I don't yet.

My girlfriend and I bump into the girl with the bicycle on

Alberta Street. She's got piercings along her lower lip, brightly colored tattoos on her neck and legs. Her ample breasts press against her sundress. They're high and round as peaches, and I hate them.

"Like her cleavage, eh?" Leanne's tone is pissed. "Maybe next time you could wait until I'm not standing right next to you."

I want to explain what I'm feeling but I'm trying to ignore this new development. I'm trying not to think about breasts, so of course they're all I see.

My father and brother pick me up at Newark airport and drive me to Sloan Kettering in New York, where I am sure I will hear a better answer.

I chose Dr. Vaughn from a lineup on the Sloan web site. She specializes in early cancer, and she looks young and attractive. I fantasize about her taking me to dinner after my appointment, telling me she's shocked at how far behind Portland doctors are regarding breast cancer. "Almost byzantine," I imagine her saying, "like they just want to cut breasts off rather than heal them."

"Your radiologist made a really good call," the real Dr. Vaughn says as she enters the examination room. "Really good. These cells are practically invisible."

Get to the good part, I'm thinking, when you tell me this whole business is crazy. What Dr. Vaughn says, though, is that my decision should depend on how I feel about risk. Both the double mastectomy, and lumpectomies and tamoxifen, are medically reasonable options. She says a whole lot more but all I hear is that I still have a choice. A Sloan Kettering doctor wouldn't let me skip out on mastectomies if my life was in danger.

"That's not exactly what she said," my father says quietly.

We are sitting in a bar in Manhattan around the corner from the hospital.

"Leave her alone," my brother says. We all sip our vodka gimlets in unison.

The day after I get back from New York I ride the #12 bus downtown to work. Through the wet trees a bright green glow spills over the narrow streets, the chrome on cars, and the cranes crowning the cityscape.

My cell phone startles me. I pull it out and see Dr. Vaughn's name. I tremble opening the phone. Perhaps a brand-new research study suggests DCIS is rarely dangerous. Maybe she's just concerned about me and wants to do dinner the next time she's in Portland.

"Jacqueline, this is Dr. Vaughn."

"Yes, hi."

"I'm glad I got you. Do you have a minute to talk?"

"Yep, just getting off the bus," and I rush off at SW 6th and Main by the Standard Insurance building, two stops early. I hurry to a stone bench near the bubbling fountain. A man with a briefcase steers around me, but I've got the phone pressed against my ear. Dr. Vaughn is going to save me from this nightmare.

"Two of our pathologists reviewed all your slides, and I wanted to explain what they found, since it contradicts what your pathologists said."

I'm ecstatic, having forgotten about the second opinion on the slides. My heart starts pounding because soon I'll be calling my girlfriend to say, baby, waiting was the right thing to do, because, guess what? I'm FINE.

"Our pathologists found significant amounts of what your pathologists called pre-cancer, in both breasts, to actually be a mixture of pre-cancer and early cancer. These irregularities—

and there are a lot of them, extending all the way to the margins—should be considered early cancer. I'll fax you the report so you can read it, too." My jaw tightens. "So now you need to disregard what I said yesterday. I'm afraid the balance has shifted. Now I'm with your surgeon. Mastectomy would definitely be the safer choice. The better one, really, if you're concerned about your health. But if you decide not to have the mastectomies, your surgeon would need to remove all of these irregularities, with clear margins. If that's possible," she adds.

"Oh."

"So. I wanted to get this information to you as soon as possible. Do you have any questions?"

"Is it possible your pathologists could be mistaken?"

Dr. Vaughn pauses.

"These are judgment calls, of course. But I for one wouldn't want you betting on our doctors being wrong." She pauses again. "I'm sorry. I'm sure this isn't what you wanted to hear."

After we hang up, I watch a crow hop across the street. I hoist my bag over my shoulder and walk to my building, ride the elevator, and disappear into my office, where even turning on the computer feels impossibly difficult. That day, I learn to type without reading, read without comprehending, comprehend without believing.

In my dreams I tear at the blouses of chesty girls. And it's not just nightmares anymore: the twenty year olds in halters in my office make me angry. It's fury and also a kind of longing. Breast envy? I start wondering if men ever experience it.

"Don't touch me there," I say to Leanne when we make love. It's the closest I come to admitting I might choose mastectomies. But having her hold back, steering her hands around my breasts, brings on more tears. I'm choosing to hold back now.

Later, Leanne says it's hard for her to talk anymore about my decision.

"You're sick of hearing about it, aren't you?" I ask, dread in my voice. I'm repetitive, analytical, indecisive. I'm unlovable.

"That's not it at all," she says firmly, holding me as always. But she doesn't say why it's hard for her. There are many things she doesn't say now, and maybe it's better.

Dr. Jones never wavers in her recommendation. Not once does she suggest we just wait and see. She doesn't vacillate even when I pull my last card, the one I believe will end this ordeal.

It is 7 p.m., when Dr. Jones usually returns my calls. After her surgeries and office visits. My phone rings and her name appears on my cell phone.

"I've thought hard about everything you've said," I start, pausing. I need to go slowly; this will change my life forever. "First I want to thank you for how much you obviously care about my health."

"You're my patient, and I care about you very much," she replies.

"I want to suggest something that may seem odd."

"OK."

"What if I don't care how my breasts look afterward? What if you remove every bit of suspicious tissue from my breasts? You just take out everything and not worry about the cosmetic result. I realize you're trying to make sure I come out of this looking normal. But what I'm trying to say is that what upsets me isn't losing my figure. It's the loss of sexual feeling. I'd rather have deformed breasts, if it means I can still have those feelings."

I expect Dr. Jones to think this over but she doesn't even pause.

"Even if we cut away all the DCIS and the areas with

potential DCIS, I'd still be worried about the breast tissue that remains."

Now I'm really quiet. I hadn't realized this wasn't about cutting away the bad cells, but not leaving any cells behind.

I do not call Dr. Jones for a while.

One morning at 3 a.m. I tell Leanne that I really have no idea how I'll make a decision. "I mean *really*," I whisper.

"Not deciding is deciding," she says firmly. She's wanted to say this, and more, for some time. And it's starting to sink in: there's yes or no, nothing in between.

I visit my oncologist again. Apparently he hadn't said I had a viable choice during our last appointment. "I always said I agreed with Dr. Jones that mastectomies would be the best decision," he says. "But then I don't have breasts, and it's your decision."

I review the evidence again and wait to hear a new voice that cries out, "Do it, for God's sake. This could be your life you're talking about." But I don't hear that voice yet.

Later, images come to me. I see myself waking up in a hospital bed, Leanne smiling down at me sweetly. Or I see myself pulling onto SW Barnes Road, then turning left into the hospital parking lot. These images are new conversations happening deep inside me, small steps toward acceptance—though I don't know that yet.

A month later my mother flies to Portland. It is the day before my surgery. When my father calls from New York, she asks to speak to him. I hand her the phone, unsure of what will follow. They've hardly spoken in twenty-five years. She sits at my teak kitchen table, propped up on her elbows, frog-legged on the chair, her back to me.

"Jacqueline looks stressed, of course, and she's got dark

circles under her eyes. I'm sure she hasn't been sleeping. To be expected, of course." She pauses. "Hard to say. No. Hard to say that, too."

I pace back and forth as my mother talks about me in the third person: "We'll get her stocked up with soft foods later today. Right now I want her to rest."

I want to scream. It's not the surgery. Maybe it's hearing the two of them talking about me. It doesn't sound like love. Maybe it just took too damn long.

I'm standing in the Portland airport on my way home from a business trip. Shouts from a boxing match blast through the speakers from all corners of the bar. Men and women sit alone at café tables, talking on cell phones.

I feel normal. My hair is longer, more like my mother's. I look "less gay," she says, mostly due to the blush and lipstick I started wearing when I looked a little peaked from the surgery. I'm being rearranged, going through a slew of strange changes to my chest, yet each day I'm a little farther along. My chest is scarred…and not perfect. Tears of gratitude fill my eyes. I've learned that healing doesn't make you perfect again. I've learned I never was—something I didn't know before coming to this unassuming city of trees near a craggy coast.

Before, I worried that I'd feel maimed. But I don't. When I breathe in deeply, staring at the setting sun as it slips beneath the tree line, I feel something strong in me. For now I call it health.

Leanne and I make love early on a Sunday morning. We are quiet as we undress. She's seen my chest many times now, but this time will be different. Neither of us looks at it, although once, as we're holding each other, I catch her smiling down at all of me.

My hands reach up to touch my breasts—something I do when I am aroused—and then of course I stop myself. She doesn't notice. And then, as I'm thinking about it, I can feel the ticklish softness there. I can even imagine how the feeling would expand and grow with the pressure mounting between my legs. It takes a little longer for me to come. Not much. I cry afterward, releasing things I haven't said out loud. The next time, or maybe the time after that, I actually look forward to that shadowy feeling. How unbelievable. I accept its presence—which is an absence—as a new companion I will come to love more each day.

The Furnace Guy
Tom Spanbauer

Septing in Portland. I always try to get through September without turning the furnace on. It never happens though. September is also the month to have the tune-up done on my furnace. That year, three years ago now, the September when the first part of this story took place, the furnace man at my door was a handsome young man named Lee.

Lee was in his late twenties, stocky, clear brown eyes and a beard. The oval patch on his blue overalls a bright red L E E. Something about Lee that was gruff, like he was trying to be a together furnace guy but underneath he was just a kid and it showed and he didn't like it. Then maybe the gruffness I sensed in Lee might have had something to do with the posters in my basement. There's the poster of Jesse Helms and Joe McCarthy that says: *separated at birth. Those who do not acknowledge the past are condemned to repeat it.* And another poster, again of Jesse Helms—a painting this time and above him are the words: *Holy Homophobia.* Then there's the clincher. The poster right next to the furnace door: QUEER NIGHT *every Monday night at La Luna.*

That's where we were standing, Lee and I, in front of the QUEER NIGHT poster, the bare light bulb hanging down, swinging a bit, casting light back and forth onto QUEER NIGHT, QUEER NIGHT, QUEER NIGHT like on the mother's skull in the basement of Hitchcock's *Psycho*.

I showed Lee the furnace switch. I showed him the furnace door. I showed him the particular detail of how the screw that held the furnace door was stripped. Then, stepping over and through all the junk I've got stashed in that corner of my basement, I finally managed to plug in the extension cord to connect his lamp. Lee turned on his lamp, undid the pesky screw to the furnace door, hung his lamp inside the guts of the furnace and started to take out his tools.

Do you need anything? I asked.

Lee didn't answer, just shook his head no.

Like I said, gruff.

On my way up the steep narrow stairs to my kitchen, I stopped. There is another door to my basement that opens out into the garden. I suggested to Lee that it might be easier for him to use the garden door to go back and forth to his truck instead of coming up the steep narrow steps and into my kitchen. Lee mumbled something. I'm not sure what. I took it to mean he'd use that door.

Upstairs was my boyfriend, Sage, straight in from Olympia. God it was great to see him. Just like that we were in a big suck face kiss and it wasn't long and we were on the bed. One thing led to another and it wasn't long and we were fully involved. The whole time while I'm making out with Sage, there's a little voice in my head that's saying, *there's a strange man downstairs and you should at least close the bedroom door.* But my lover was persistent. After a long kiss that started on my mouth and then went all the way to my ear, I managed: "The furnace guy is downstairs. His name is Lee."

Sage took his mouth off my ear, pulled back and looked at me. "Is he cute?"

That made us laugh. All of a sudden we were in one of those bad porn movies where the hunky furnace guy catches the two men fucking upstairs.

"Yes," I said.

Sage and I are a lot alike. When we make love we both want the blind closed during the day, and at night, if the window is open, the lights turned off. Don't get me wrong, we're not ashamed of our bodies, or ashamed of being gay. We're not overly modest, or hung up on Christian morality.

Yet again, I guess we are hung up. Both Sage and I were raised in weird Catholic families. And you don't come out of Catholicism sexually unscathed. But I don't see us any more fucked up than anybody else growing up in America, or anywhere else for that matter. I mean sex is so personal and complex. How can you escape not having ghosts in your sexuality?

Plus, I'd have to say that there is a bit of an exhibitionist in me. I'm an old hippy who's spent a lot of his life getting naked. And that wasn't easy, it was hard work, getting naked. I was born in the late forties, and learning to feel somewhat comfortable naked in my pock-marked Catholic skin for other people's eyes was a real liberation. I'm proud of my naked body. I mean mostly. These days though I'm dealing with being sixty-two years old. All that body image shit I had to work through all those years seems to be starting all over again now that I'm aging. Shoulders back, chest up, gut sucked in. I swear it's a vicious cycle.

Still, even these days, often in the morning, I'll open the drapes in my birthday suit. I mean I'm careful about it. I open the left drape while I'm standing behind the right, and if the coast is clear, I open the right. I don't get off standing naked in my front room window.

Sage would never open the blinds naked. But he's much less inhibited than I in other situations. For example, Fairy Gatherings are not known for their Puritanism. And Sage spends a lot of time at Fairy Gatherings. Sage's photos from these gatherings are lots of naked men and naked women standing next to super heroes in full costume and Barbra Streisand and Jackie Kennedy and big bunny rabbits and guys with bones in their noses and Prince Alberts through their dicks.

Then there's my secret inner voyeur. I guess I've always liked to watch. Must see, must look, must know has been the chant since I was a kid. This secret voyeuristic desire found its full blooming during my years in New York City. I became an avid window watcher. Don't get me wrong. I'm not a Peeping Tom. Well, I mean I am, but I didn't like sneak up and look into people's windows in the hopes of catching them doing dirty things. Just walking by on the street, if I saw someone through their window, something almost holy would come over me, and I would have to stop and stare. A woman washing dishes. Men in suits, women in cocktail dresses having a party. A man without a shirt doing jumping jacks. A man sitting in a big chair and reading in a glow of light. Whatever it was the person was doing, it all seemed somehow to be happening in capital letters. A WOMAN WASHING DISHES. MEN IN SUITS, WOMEN IN COCKTAIL DRESSES HAVING A PARTY. A MAN WITHOUT A SHIRT DOING JUMPING JACKS. A MAN SITTING IN A BIG CHAIR READING IN A GLOW OF LIGHT.

Oh! The Humanity! It was overwhelming.

Usually if I sensed that the person I was watching knew I was watching, I lost interest. Yet I had a neighbor on East Fifth Street who had no shades or curtains on his windows. His building was a smaller building behind the building where

I had an apartment. His windows were huge and I had full view of his east wall and his south wall. I saw every damn thing that guy ever did except take a shit. The first weeks in that apartment, when I watched him, I made sure he couldn't see me. I hovered behind Venetian blinds with the lights off in my apartment. But that soon changed. I don't know when it happened, or how, but after months living along side of him, he became like the subway noise—constantly there. He *and* his girl friends. Then one night, rolling my naked self into bed, I turned off the light and there he was, standing at his window watching me. Big smile on his face. After that, that was just how it was with me and him. It was a strange intimacy.

All this is going around in my head and more and who knows what all is going on in Sage's head as we're taking off our shirts, pulling down our pants and all the while down in the basement is Lee, the Furnace Guy. I try not to think that he's down there. I haven't seen my boyfriend in a week and it's just so great to be in Sage's arms again and our love making has nothing to do with the sexy Furnace Guy who just happens to be in my basement at the moment. And just who is this Lee? Does he like to watch? Is that why he decided to become a Furnace repairman, so he could go in people's houses and listen to them fuck in the next room? Or is he still back way before the sixties and seventies ever happened—is he still lost in some Christian ideal of propriety? And if he catches us, oh fuck, I hope he doesn't think we wanted him to catch us, because that would be so tacky. Yet there he is, down in the basement with his lamp, banging on the furnace vents, dropping his pliers, and we're naked on the bed. Neither one of us, Sage and I, want to accidentally make some noise to give a clue to Lee the Furnace Guy that there are two grown men just a couple of feet above him, rapidly being reduced into one squirming Francis Bacon body in fragrante delecto.

And neither one of us, Sage or I, get up and close the bedroom door.

Just past Sage's ear and over his bare shoulder, just beyond the bulk of Sage's naked body lying all mixed up with my naked body on the bed, beyond that the edge of the bed, beyond, the three feet to the door of the bedroom, and beyond, at the door to the bedroom, stands a very shocked and very confused Furnace Guy, Lee.

"I have to check the thermostat," Lee says. It sounds like an apology. Lee's voice is not gruff. His voice sounds like a little boy's voice, whose feelings have been hurt.

The thermostat. The fucking thermostat. Of course, the fucking Furnace Guy has got to check the fucking thermostat. Fuck.

Lee the Furnace Guy ducks into the front room where the thermostat is.

Then he has to stand in the front room, turn on the thermostat, wait there until the furnace clicks on, and when the furnace clicks on, which it probably would, *then* Lee the Furnace guy has to walk past the bedroom door *again* to get back to the basement.

At this point, I get up and close the bedroom door.

Sage and I lie on the bed. We don't move. We're trying not to be Catholic. We're hoping that Lee knocks on the door. We're hoping that he does not.

We are at the back door, Lee and I. I have all my clothes on. Lee says nothing about the two naked men having sex he's just seen. I am taking deep breaths. Part of me is trying not to feel like a naughty boy. Part of me won't admit that the whole thing even happened. Part of me wants to giggle and hold my head and scream fuck fuck fuck. Part of me is trying to get Lee to look me directly in the eye because I want to look back—show him that even though I feel like a damn fool, I'm proud to be a queer man who made a choice, and whether it was bad choice or a good choice, I was going to stick by it. Stick by me. Another part of me is just watching.

Lee says, "My mother caught me jerking off behind the garage when I was fourteen."

Lee says, "Wow it was weird seeing two naked men embracing. I've never seen that before. I was so shocked."

Lee says, "It's the body hair that's so different. I'm so used to the smooth skin of women."

Lee says, "Yah, me and my boyfriend like to have sex in the car while we're passing trucks on the freeway."

Lee says, "You know that if this was in Iraq or Iran, you two would be in deep shit right now."

Lee says, "You know if this were just about any country in the world outside the U.S. and Europe, you two would be in deep shit right now."

Lee says, "You know if this were Idaho or Mississippi or Texas or any of the red states, you two would be in deep shit right now."

Lee says, "You know if this were Roseburg, Oregon instead of Portland, Oregon, you two could be in deep shit right now."

Lee says, "You know you put me in an awkward position and it pissed me off."

Lee says, "I'm just a guy trying to get his job done. Do you know how many more jobs I have waiting for me today?"

Lee says, "You fags are all alike. You're all going to hell. You're fucking disgusting."

Lee says, "You know what you do in the privacy of your home is up to you, but that's what it is, *private.* "

Lee says, "I ought to kick your ass."

Lee says, "I tell you what. I'll fuck your boyfriend while you suck him off."

Lee says, "I feel tricked into something I don't want any part of."

Lee says, "If it would have been you and your girlfriend, now that would have been a different story."

Lee says, "Or two girlfriends."

Lee says, "One man one woman, no problem."

Lee says all of the above.

But really Lee says nothing. Lee is back to being gruff, real gruff and all business. So I'm all business too. I sign the receipt and write out the check. Lee tears off the pink slip of the receipt and hands it to me. In writing class I always tell my students that when an object is exchanged to make sure and slow the writing down because the object is not only an object but an embodiment of energy flowing directly from one person to another. So I let the moment stay open for whatever could fill it. But Lee's face has become a mask of his face and the object of the pink receipt stays a pink receipt and nothing else, and that nothing else is the way Lee wants things to be. He'll have it no other way.

One year later it's September and the second part of this story. I try to get through September without turning on my furnace. But I have to turn on my furnace. September the month that I get the tune up on my furnace. This year in fact, I need a *new* furnace. The furnace man at my door is a sexy young man named Lee. Red letters on the blue overalls L E E.

The same Lee.

Lee is gruff the way he was gruff last year but this time his gruff has something else to it. It's a smirk. A you-can't-fool-me-this-time smirk. A I'm-on-to-you smirk. A I-dare-you-to-run-that-by-me-again smirk. And something else. In this moment,

Lee is the one who is doing the watching. He watches my face go *what the fuck*. He watches me catch my breath. He watches and is aware of the moment the way *I* made myself aware the last time.

In the basement, it's the posters. Jesse Helms and Joe McCarthy. Jesse Helms *Holy Homophobia*. Queer Night Queer Night Queer Night. I go through all my junk in that corner of the basement and finally get Lee's lamp plugged in. Lee's got the pesky screw undone and the furnace door off and he's just hung his lamp in the guts of the furnace when I ask: "I think it's time I bought a new furnace, what do you say?"

There's a long gruff pause. So long, in fact, that I think he hasn't heard me.

"This furnace is over twenty years old," I say. "Do you think it can make it through another year?"

Still nothing. I'm about to ask again, when, as gruff as he can make it, and with the smirk, Lee says, "I'm just the furnace repair guy. You'll have to call up and talk to a sales rep for that information."

"OK," I said. "But I'm interested. What do you think?"

It was a question that only at that moment did I realize all the ways it could be answered. And Lee knew it. He knew all the ways. And he knew I knew. And he took his sweet time.

"Like I said," he said, "I'm only the repairman. Best to call up a sales rep."

So I go up my steep narrow staircase and call the furnace company. The woman who answers the phone has a voice that sounds like a cute little girl. "Jones Heating and Air Conditioning. This is Melanie. How can I make you smile?"

Every September when I call Jones Heating and Air Conditioning this woman answers. Every time it's the same thing. I'm always at a loss for words because what kind of grown woman would talk with a voice like that? And what the fuck is *how can I make you smile* about? She's so cheery and perky the first thing I think is that she's being ironic and I think I've misdialed and got some phone sex line.

Finally, last September, I said, "Don't say that."

She said, "Say what?"

"How can I make you smile?" I said, "Don't say that. In fact, you can't make me smile."

That put a hurt tone into Melanie's little girl voice and then she started in: It was just a common courtesy, they were a friendly company, she was just doing her job, promoting good will, being positive, bringing a little piece of light into people's lives, and on and on. Really, there was no arguing with her. She was Melanie and she could make me smile because this was, well, this was America and we look on the bright side of things in America.

"What about irony?" I said.

Melanie didn't get it, irony.

So on *this* particular September, I was ready for Melanie. And when Melanie answered, when Melanie said, "Good afternoon. Jones Heating and Air Conditioning, this is Melanie. How can I make you smile?" I just say in my own sweet little voice, "Thank you so much Melanie, but I don't want to smile, let me talk to your sales department."

Irony. Oh say can you see?

As soon as Melanie switches me over to the sales department I can tell that something has gone wrong. At first I think she didn't make the connection correctly, then as I wait to see what has actually happened, I can hear two voices talking. The two voices are Melanie and another woman. And they don't know I'm listening.

Other woman: "You know who that is, don't you? Spanbauer?

Melanie: "Yes, he's a grouch."

Other woman: "No, no. He's a fag. Last year Lee caught him making out with his boyfriend."

Melanie: "Eeeeuuuwww!"

Other Woman: "Two men naked on the bed, kissing and rubbing each other, can you imagine?"

Melanie: "Eeeuuuwww! Gross!"

The conversation kept going but I'd heard enough. I began to yell into the phone: "Melanie! Melanie! I can hear every word you're saying! This is that faggot Spanbauer and I can hear every word you're saying!"

There was an immediate click and the line went dead.

Five minutes later my phone rang.

It wasn't Melanie. It was another woman, maybe *the* other woman, and she said, "This is So and So from Jones Heating and Air Conditioning."

I knew I had them by the balls. My rage was self-righteous and finely tuned. I had caught *them* with their pants down—and then there was the issue of the five thousand dollar new furnace I wanted to buy. I started meta and went micro. I said something like this: "It's difficult being queer in this society. Queer people have to put up with so much prejudice. You have no idea the effect that homophobia has on our lives. Self respect isn't something you're born with and with gay people it is something they consciously have to learn and then practice every day. And here I am, just this guy calling up his furnace company to buy a new furnace and what do I get but some office gossip about an event that was absolutely mortifying to me. Well, you can forget about that furnace. I am taking my business somewhere where I will be respected and appreciated."

And I hung up the phone.

Lee was in the basement. I thought about going into the

bedroom and closing the door and when Lee came up to check the thermostat, I'd make loud sex noises of astonishing satisfaction.

But then the phone rang again. This time it was Melanie. She was crying so hard she could barely talk. "Oh, Mr. Spanbauer. I am so sorry. It was just the two of us in the office here and we didn't think anyone could hear. We meant no harm."

"But you called me a fag," I said.

Melanie's lament went an octave higher. "Oh we're so sorry Mr. Spanbauer. We won't ever let it happen again. As a token of our deep appreciation for your business we at Jones Heating and Air Conditioning would like to offer you a free duct cleaning."

My last discussion with Melanie about irony had gone nowhere. But I couldn't resist.

"Melanie," I said, "Do you know how ridiculous *duct cleaning* sounds after that conversation of yours I just overheard?"

A big gasp of sucked in air on Melanie's side of the phone. "I know I know!" she cried, "They made me say it."

When I went downstairs, Lee was on his cell phone. He was just finishing up. He handed me the papers. I signed on the dotted line. Lee tore off the pink copy and handed it to me. There it was that moment again when you slow things down. I thought maybe I'd say something about Sage and me naked on the bed the year before. Say I was sorry. Or tell him I'd totally forgotten about the thermostat, or something. Just say something about what happened so it could exist in the air between us. But I waited too long, the moment passed, and I didn't say a thing.

The Lesbian Lexicon
Presented by Stevie Anntonym

biodude *n.* a biological dude.

boycation *n.* a brief period wherein a dyke dates a biodude to take a break from gayland and gay drama; can result in a reaffirmation of how really super gay she actually is.

bros *n. pl.* lesbian-identified individuals who bond socially over activities like videogames, board games, sports events, pizza dinners, teenage mutant ninja turtles, etc. *n.* **bromance** bro activities accompanied by feelings of romance. *adj.* **bromantic**. *n.* **bromosexual** bros who are sexually attracted to other bros.

dildon'ts *pl. n.* anything that takes the fun out of playing with toys.

dopplebanger *n.* one who only fucks people who have an uncanny resemblance to themselves.

dutchboy *n.* the male equivalent of a fag hag—the guy who hangs out around dykes.

fagnet *n.* a straight woman beloved by gay men.

fagosphere *n.* an environment dominated by fags.

fauxfag *n.* a straight boy who has intentionally cultivated a fabulously faggy aesthetic, often to the express advantage of bedding those ladies who get crushes on their fag friends because they are considered "safe."

fauxmo *n.* (rhymes with homo) a fake homo.

F2Minist *n.* a fella who KEEPS IT REAL 'cause he understands that externalizing internalized misogyny looks tacky in any gender, remembers his own lesbian feminist roots (if he had any), and resists the urge to become a tranny chauvinist.

frienemy *n.* a person who can't stand you, has your worst intentions at heart, laughs bitterly at every little humiliation life throws your way as if it is personal vindication from a vengeful god...yet remains ruthlessly friendly to your face.

Highlander Femme *n.* a femme who has that "There Can Only Be One" attitude towards other femmes; prefers to surround herself with a hive of masculine-gendered people and loyal ex-lovers; will allow the occasional lesser femme into her orbit but only if they willingly submit to Her Most Excellent and are good little helpers.

housewreck *v.* to sleep with two or more people of the same household, causing one or more persons to move out, give up the lease, or leave town.

lovejail *n.* a very special and remote place some couples reside in during the first few months to a year after falling in love; a place wherein all interest in friends, family, hobbies, employment, the weather, and current events are diminished; a place from which it is difficult to return phone calls.

Mr.McToppity *n.* one who is a top on the streets as well as in the sheets, and proudly so.

otherfucker *n.* a person only attracted to people of differing gender expressions than themselves. *antonym:* dopplebanger.

pronoun showdown *n.* a conversation between two people about a third party in which two differing pronouns are being pointedly used by each participant (as if in a duel) and without any acknowledgement of this discrepancy in a subtle battle of who's got the right gender.

Sexual Tension Disorder (STD) *n.* a condition in which a person lives with Prince in their very own erotic city; a state in which someone's general presence exudes a panty-load of undirected sexual energy, regardless of the circumstance.

textual intercourse *n.* sexxxy smut sent via text message.

trannyhopper *n.* a person who dates tranny after tranny after tranny.

whatever-the-fuck-I-want-gomy *n.* the practice of doing whatever the fuck one wants while pretending they are in a consensual, polyamorous (or monogamous) relationship.

Contributors

Marc Acito's comic debut novel, *How I Paid for College: A Novel of Sex, Theft, Friendship and Musical Theater* won the Ken Kesey Award and made the American Library Association's Top Ten Teen Book List. It was also selected as an Editors' Choice by the *New York Times* and is translated into five languages the author does not read. The eagerly anticipated sequel, *Attack of the Theater People*, was selected as a top read for 2008 by the Seattle Public Library. Marc is now a regular commentator on National Public Radio's *All Things Considered*. His first play, *Holidazed*, which he co-wrote with C.S. Whitcomb, received its world premiere at Artists Repertory Theatre in Portland.

Trans writer **Jacob Anderson-Minshall** co-authors the *Blind Eye Mystery* series with his co-conspirator, Diane (Editor in Chief of *Curve* magazine). He co-hosts Gender Blender on KBOO 90.7 fm. Jacob freelances with *Bitch* and *Just Out*, has pieces in several anthologies including *Men Speak Out*, and authored the syndicated column TransNation from 2005-2009.

Stevie Anntonym is a gay word nerd. Contributors to The Lesbian Lexicon include Donna Potts, Vera, Nicole J. Georges, sts, Winner, Freddy Fagula, Leah H, Jules, Stacy Cottler,

Amanda, Kayan, Valentine, Hope, Lois Leveen, Spencer Bergstedt, Kathleen Bryson, Leopold, Stevie Ann, Florence Card, and Ill. Email your words: lesbianlexicon@yahoo.com.

Lynn Barkley lives in Portland with her partner and their two sons. She loves the outdoors, her partner, and her sons.

Kathleen Bryson is the author of two novels, *Mush* (Diva Books, 2001) and *Girl on a Stick* (Suspect Thoughts Press, 2008). Born and raised in Alaska, she has degrees in anthropology, Swedish, and film. As a painter and performer, she has had eight solo art exhibitions, played Hawaiian slide guitar in the laziest Riot Grrl band in history, and acted in more than twenty short films, most recently as blonde bombshell Diana Dors in "I Am Diana Dors." Her feature film directorial debut, "The Viva Voce Virus," started its festival run in November, 2008. Her website: www.spaceshipsovercorvallis.com.

David Ciminello is the author of the feature film "Bruno" (2000). His fiction has appeared in the literary journal *Lumina*, his poetry in *Poetry Northwest*. He currently lives and writes in New York City.

Sarah Dougher has been working as a musician, writer and teacher for over fifteen years. She teaches at Portland State University, and works at p:ear, an organization committed to the emotional, physical and intellectual well-being of homeless and transitional young people in downtown Portland. Additionally, she runs the Flash Choir, and has released eight records on independent labels.

sts lives at 19th St. House in Portland. For many years, she wrote the zine *Way Down Low*, played drums for The Haggard,

Shemo, and Cadallaca, and made short movies including "The Lesbian Movie 2000." She currently works at the Rock 'n' Roll Camp for Girls and plays goalie for a women's futsol team called Chainsaw Parade.

Dexter Flowers started her writing career as an eighth grade advice columnist. Since then, she's busted out in the 2007 national Sister Spit tour and is published in the anthologies *Baby Remember My Name* and *It's So You*, both edited by Michelle Tea. She's been a featured reader at the San Francisco library's RADAR reading series, run a slew of open mics, and has a zine called *Maybe It's Something You Ate* co-created with Sarah Gottesdiener. She spends most of her time digging up awkward stories from her childhood, and performing with her band Seagull and Wave. She is currently recording a spoken word CD with Radio Sloan.

Sarah Gottesdiener is a queer artist and musician living in Portland. Click to www.sarahfaith.com.

After nearly fifty years, **Wayne Gregory** realized that being true to self is what's important. He believes that life will amaze us with the small things and that writing is a spiritual endeavor that uncovers who we are and connects us with things larger than ourselves. He's from southern Louisiana where the air is hot, the food spicy, and religion thick as swamp fog. He's a father of six, grandfather of three, and a teacher of linguistics.

Megan Kruse's work has appeared in *Oyez Review, Bellingham Review, Fiddlehead, Oregon Literary Review, Phoebe, Gertrude,* and *Vespertine Press*. She's the recipient of residency grants from the Kimmel Harding Nelson Center in Nebraska and the Ragdale Foundation of Illinois, as well as an Oregon Literary

Arts Fellowship. Currently an MFA student at the University of Montana, she is at work on a collection of short fiction.

Tony Longshanks LeTigre believes in human evolution and is happy to be along for the ride. He is graduating from Portland State University with a major in Arts and Letters and a minor in Spanish. He has also attended the University of Minnesota and The Evergreen State College, ushered for Cirque du Soleil, and hobnobbed with the rich and flaming. Tony believes that the only real sins are meekness, modesty, and lack of humor.

Lois Leveen learned more from the drag queens in her dorm than from all her college professors. After forays in the other queer meccas of North America, she has settled in lesbiriffic Portland, where she lives in a bright green house called Dutchboy. Her creative work has appeared in *Bitch*, *Oregon Literary Review*, the Richard Foreman Festival, the Olympia Film Festival, the Boston Underground Film Festival, and on the NPR show LiveWire. Read her blog at http://macaronimaniac. blogspot.com. For "My Other Mother is Also a Lesbian" T-shirts, visit www.cafepress.com/macaronimaniac.

Donal Mosher's fiction and nonfiction have appeared in *Instant City*, *Satellite*, *Frozen Tears*, and *Still Blue*, an anthology of working class writing. His photo book collaboration with Canadian writer Derek McCormac is forthcoming from Artspace Books. The documentary film "October Country" is based on his photography. He is also a principle subject of Robert Arnold's ITVS documentary film "Key of G," which focuses on life and work with a severely disabled young man.

Annie Murphy is a comics artist, illustrator, and queer-bird-watcher born and raised in Portland. She contributed a suit to the *Collective Tarot* (a radical queer tarot deck), co-conspired on the comics anthology *Group Sex Comics*, and received a Xeric award for her graphic novella *I Still Live: Biography of a Spiritualist.*

J.T. Neel is an escape artist from a tiny place where the Midwest meets the South. A writer of autobiographical fiction, fantastical truth, and the occasional love letter, J.T. is a member of a queer writing collective in Portland.

David Oates writes nonfiction and poetry about urban and natural topics. "Unlocking the Hips" is from his forthcoming book *What We Love Will Save Us.* Previous books include *City Limits: Walking Portland's Boundary* (2006), *Paradise Wild: Reimagining American Nature* (2003), and *Peace in Exile: Poems* (1992). Click to davidoates.info.

Like every good dyke, **Christa Orth** read Leslie Feinberg's *Stone Butch Blues* and was inspired by the intersections between queer rights and workers' rights. She's been asking folks to tell their work stories ever since. A teacher and historian, she now lives in Brooklyn, New York.

Jacqueline Raphael has published in *Spoon River Poetry Review* and *Apostrophe* and co-authored *Writing Together: How to Transform Your Writing in a Writing Group* (Perigee, 1997). She won first place in the 2006 Portland Wordstock Festival Writing Challenge and is currently at work on a novel.

When not running his private tattoo salon in southeast Portland, **Michael Sage Ricci** teaches writing workshops with Dangerous Writers and Writers In The Schools. His work has appeared in numerous zines including *Zuni Mountain Gazette,*

The Rad-Dish, White Crane Journal, and *RadicalFaeireDigest.* He edited *Under A Silver Sky,* a 2003 anthology of Northwest Poets. His travels (professional, physical, and intellectual) have included Hawaiian and Polynesian myth and tattoo history, Comic Book esoterica, Permaculture eco-village design in rural North Carolina, painting murals and theatrical sets professionally in New York and for the casino industry, being a field instructor for at-risk teens at the School of Urban and Wilderness Survival in Idaho, and tattooing and teaching workshops nationally.

Gabrielle Rivera was born and raised in the Bronx. Landing an internship in Portland was one of the coolest things that ever happened to her. In Portland she met solid individuals who followed their own funky beat and lived life the way they saw fit. She lived as a vegetarian and chilled and learned from people who lived in communities where they grew their own food and pooled their resources to sustain their living environments. She recently wrote and directed her first independent short, "Spanish Girls are Beautiful."

Colleen Siviter is a femme-identified Deep Lez writer, stylist, traveler, visual artist, and all around creative instigator. Her inspiration stems from radical loving, fashion, tree rings, collaborations, hot dance moves, spirit guides, and the beauty of paying attention. She has a degree in magazine journalism and is working on a book of short travel-inspired stories.

Tom Spanbauer is the author of four novels: *Faraway Places, The Man Who Fell In Love With The Moon, In the City of Shy Hunters,* and *Now Is the Hour. Faraway Places* has just been reissued in a beautiful new paperback from Hawthorne Books. He teaches Dangerous Writing.

Nicole Vaicunas is a slacker extraordinaire who spends her days slaving away to The Man. By night, she dreams of being a lethal blank page assassin.